WARNING!
THESE ITEMS ARE ALL MISSING FROM THIS BOOK.
AF291336
THE MONA LISA'S LEGS
COUNT DRACULA'S SUN LAMP
PINOCCHIO'S FRESH HANDKERCHIEF
BO PEEP'S SHEEP
THE SPHINX'S NOSE
THIS CENTIPEDE'S ONE ODD SOCK
KING KONG'S CROWN
THEY ARE
NOT MARVELLOUS.
THEY ARE JUST SILLY!

A TEMPLAR BOOK

First published in the UK in 2026 by Templar Books,
an imprint of Bonnier Books UK
5th Floor, HYLO, 105 Bunhill Row,
London, EC1Y 8LZ
The authorised representative in the EEA
is Bonnier Books UK (Ireland) Limited.
Registered office address:
Block B, The Crescent Building
Northwood, Santry
Dublin 9, D09 C6X8, Ireland
compliance@bonnierbooks.ie
www.bonnierbooks.co.uk

10 9 8 7 6 5 4 3 2 1

ISBN 978-1-78342-525-9

This book was typeset in Providence Sans,
Bokka, Chubby Chap, Mind Boggle, Cookie Crumble,
1589_Humane_Bordeaux, Abril Display
The illustrations were created digitally.
Edited by Sophie Hallam and Rachael Roberts
Fact-checked by Corinne Lucas
Designed by Anna Ring
Production by Neil Randles

Printed in China

THE WORLD'S LAST MAMMOTH

AND OTHER MISSING MARVELS

MIKE BARFIELD

FRANZISKA HÖLLBACHER

CONTENTS

☆ FEATURING ☆
ALEXANDER THE GREAT
ON PAGE 16

☆ FEATURING ☆
GENGHIS KHAN
ON PAGE 26

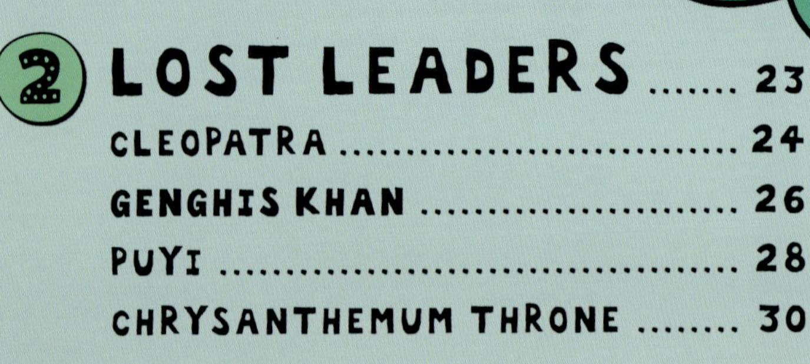

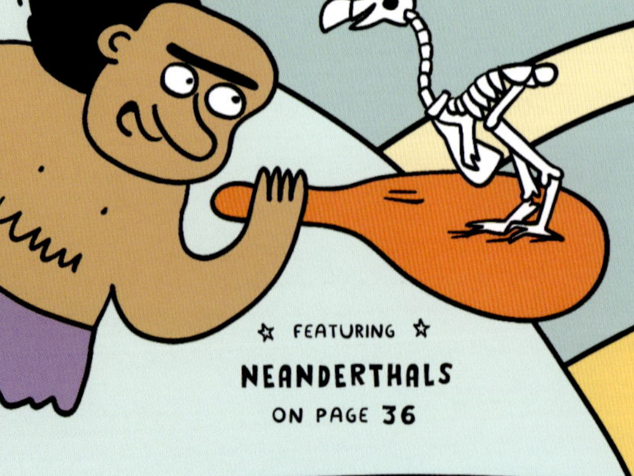

☆ FEATURING ☆
NEANDERTHALS
ON PAGE 36

☆ FEATURING ☆
AMELIA EARHART
ON PAGE 46

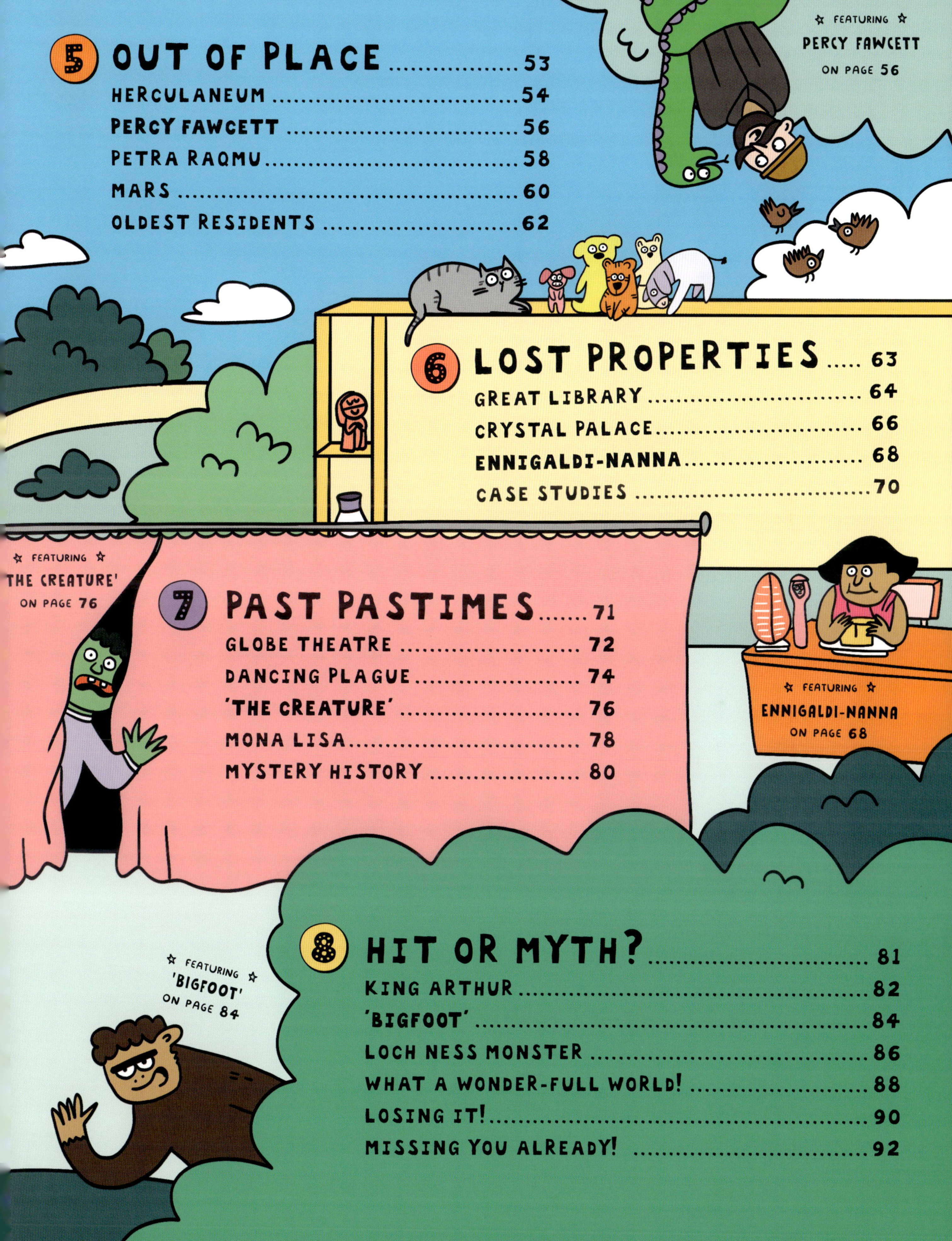

☆ FEATURING ☆
PERCY FAWCETT
ON PAGE 56

☆ FEATURING ☆
'THE CREATURE'
ON PAGE 76

☆ FEATURING ☆
ENNIGALDI-NANNA
ON PAGE 68

☆ FEATURING ☆
'BIGFOOT'
ON PAGE 84

INTRODUCTION

THE MAGNIFICENT SEVEN

The Seven Wonders of the Ancient World were mighty monuments dating back to times of togas and sandals. Only one has survived until today. In this opening chapter, we revisit the missing six and reveal the one remaining wonder. But first, here are four famous world wonders the ancient Greeks and Romans rather rudely overlooked!

MOST FAMOUS STONES

Stonehenge on Salisbury Plain in the UK was built over 4,000 years ago as a huge calendar (we think!), but you couldn't hang it on your wall!

WONDER WALL

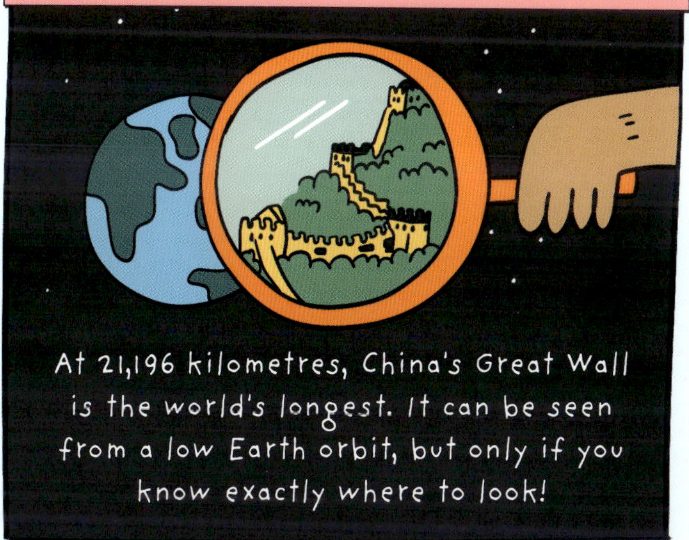

At 21,196 kilometres, China's Great Wall is the world's longest. It can be seen from a low Earth orbit, but only if you know exactly where to look!

WORLD'S LARGEST MONOLITH

Uluru, in almost the centre of Australia, is a single sandstone rock about 3 kilometres long that is sacred to the local indigenous people.

WORLD'S BIGGEST PYRAMID

Not in Egypt but in Mexico, the pyramid Tlachihualtepetl, built by the Aztec people using bricks made of air-dried mud, is the biggest by volume!

HANGING GARDENS

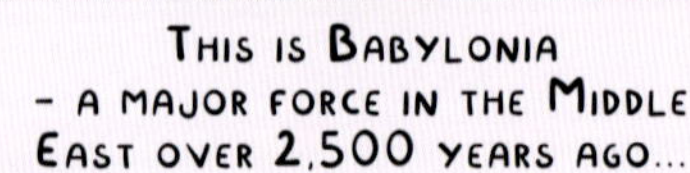

JUST GROW UP!

FRONDS IN HIGH PLACES

Not far from Mount Everest, Nepal's National Botanical Gardens are on the roof of the world, not the roof of a building. Located in the Kathmandu valley, they are home to the Spiny Babbler, a bird thought to be extinct for over 100 years until it was spotted again in the 1940s.

PITCHED ROOF

Today, the world's largest rooftop garden is above government offices in Sejong City, South Korea. The size of 11 football pitches, it is planted with over a million trees — roughly one for every resident of the city.

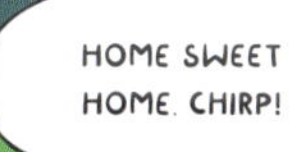

TREE-MENDOUS!

Finished in 2000, Die Waldspirale ('The Wooded-Spiral') in Darmstadt, Germany is a block of flats with a rooftop forest of trees winding its way up 12 floors. The building has over 1,000 windows — none of them the same size or shape, as the architect hated straight lines.

MOUNT PLEASANT

Opened in 1995, ACROS Fukuoka is a green mountain — just like Babylon's Hanging Gardens — in the centre of Fukuoka City, Japan. The planted terraces are a beautiful green solution to keeping the building behind them nice and cool to work in.

TEMPLE OF ARTEMIS

PAST AND PRESENT
HOLY AMAZING!

HOLE STOREY

The Pantheon in Rome was built by Emperor Hadrian between 118 and 125 CE. Its 43-metre-wide roof is the largest unsupported concrete dome in the world and has stood for over 1,900 years, despite a huge hole at the top that lets in rain!

HIGHER SPIRE

The Sagrada Família in Barcelona, Spain is the world's largest unfinished Catholic church. Its main architect, Antoni Gaudí, died in 1926, and when his unusual design is finally completed, perhaps by 2034, it should have the world's tallest spire, at 172.5 metres tall.

WAT A SIZE!

Angkor Wat in Cambodia, Southeast Asia, is the world's biggest religious structure. Built as a Hindu temple and completed in 1150 CE, it became a Buddhist site soon afterwards. Around 230 football pitches in size, the temple only became known outside Asia in the 1860s.

TURKISH DELIGHT

The Hagia Sophia in Istanbul, Türkiye, was the world's largest cathedral for nearly 1,000 years after its completion in 537 CE. Now a mosque, legend has it that columns from the Temple of Artemis were used to build it, but none have been found.

TWO STATUES

HI! WELCOME TO GREECE OVER 1,000 YEARS AGO – I'M A HEAD PIGEON...
COO!

THAT IS, I PREFER TO SIT ON THE HEADS OF STATUES, NOT OTHER PARTS.
COO!
COO, TOO!

BACK IN ANCIENT TIMES, MY ANCESTORS WERE BIG FANS OF THIS GUY, PHIDIAS, A FAMOUS SKILLED SCULPTOR...
NO STANDING STILL WHEN IT COMES TO CARVING STATUES.
CHIP!
CARVE!

AROUND 435 BCE, HE CREATED A 13-METRE-HIGH SEATED STATUE OF THE THUNDER GOD ZEUS.
SWOON!
IT'S ONE OF THE SEVEN WONDERS!
I NEED TO SIT DOWN MYSELF.

IT WAS IN A TEMPLE IN OLYMPIA, THE SITE OF THE ORIGINAL OLYMPIC GAMES...
WHOEVER BUILT THIS DESERVES A MEDAL!

MADE OF GOLD AND IVORY, THE STATUE VANISHED AROUND THE 5TH CENTURY.
IS THAT SEAT TAKEN?
NO, ONLY THE STATUE.

A SECOND STAR STATUE WAS A 32-METRE-HIGH BRONZE FIGURE OF THE SUN GOD HELIOS ON THE GREEK ISLAND OF RHODES.
I'M ON YOUR HEAD, SUN GOD!
COO, AGAIN!

COMPLETED AROUND 280 BCE, PEOPLE TRAVELLED FROM AFAR TO HONOUR THIS SO-CALLED COLOSSUS OF RHODES.
I'M A SUN WORSHIPPER.
ME TOO!

BUT IT FELL OVER AFTER AN EARTHQUAKE IN 226 BCE.
TOPPLE!
EEK! I HAVEN'T GOT A LEG TO STAND ON!
CRACK!

IT LAY THERE FOR MORE THAN 800 YEARS WHILE PEOPLE PLUNDERED THE BRONZE...
PANT!
EVEN HIS LITTLE TOE IS COLOSSAL!
PUFF!

AND, BIT BY BIT, THE ENTIRE THING DISAPPEARED.
I PREFERRED STANDING ON HIS HEAD TO THIS.
IT'S A BUM DEAL.

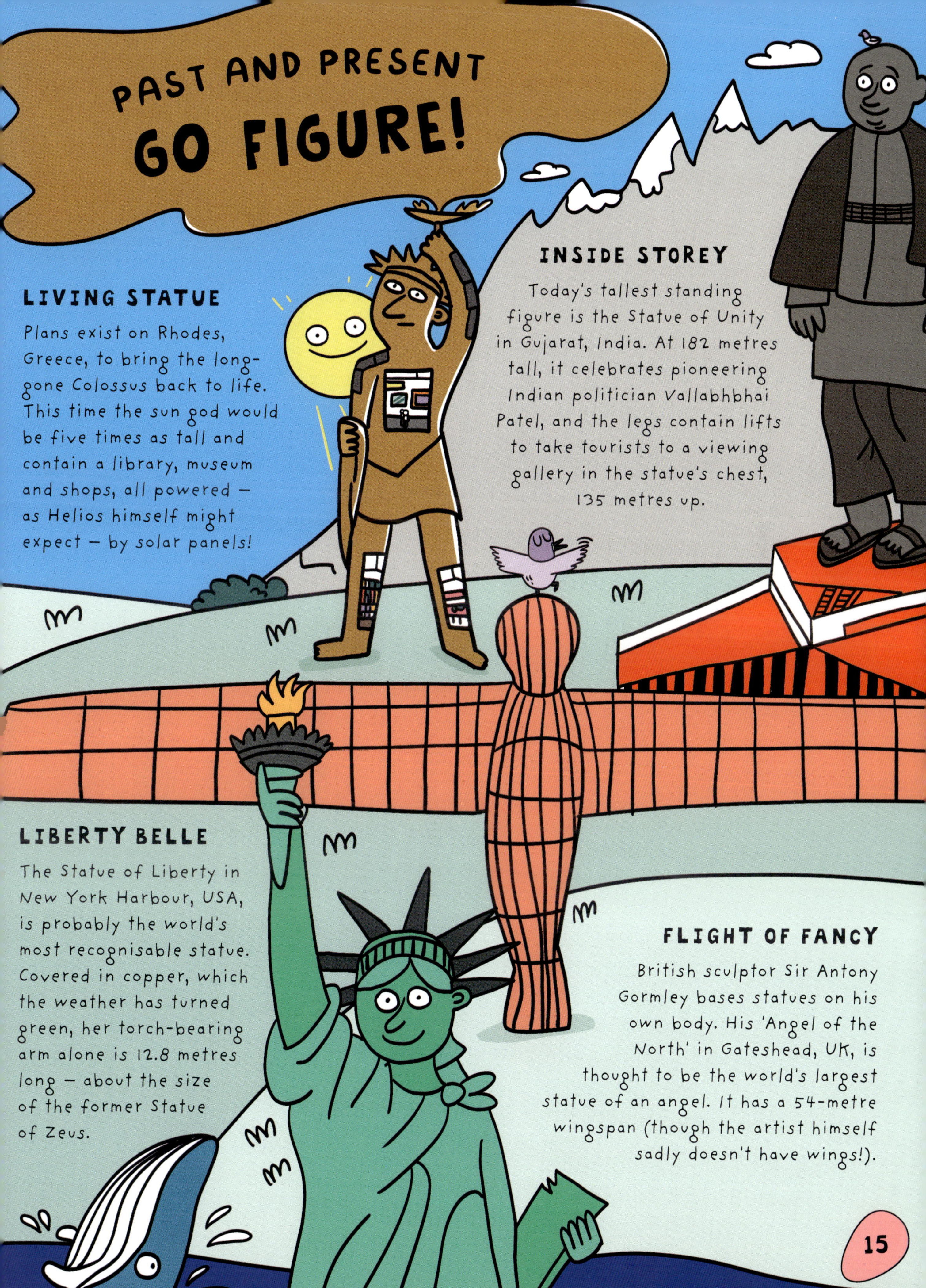

LIVING STATUE

Plans exist on Rhodes, Greece, to bring the long-gone Colossus back to life. This time the sun god would be five times as tall and contain a library, museum and shops, all powered — as Helios himself might expect — by solar panels!

INSIDE STOREY

Today's tallest standing figure is the Statue of Unity in Gujarat, India. At 182 metres tall, it celebrates pioneering Indian politician Vallabhbhai Patel, and the legs contain lifts to take tourists to a viewing gallery in the statue's chest, 135 metres up.

LIBERTY BELLE

The Statue of Liberty in New York Harbour, USA, is probably the world's most recognisable statue. Covered in copper, which the weather has turned green, her torch-bearing arm alone is 12.8 metres long — about the size of the former Statue of Zeus.

FLIGHT OF FANCY

British sculptor Sir Antony Gormley bases statues on his own body. His 'Angel of the North' in Gateshead, UK, is thought to be the world's largest statue of an angel. It has a 54-metre wingspan (though the artist himself sadly doesn't have wings!).

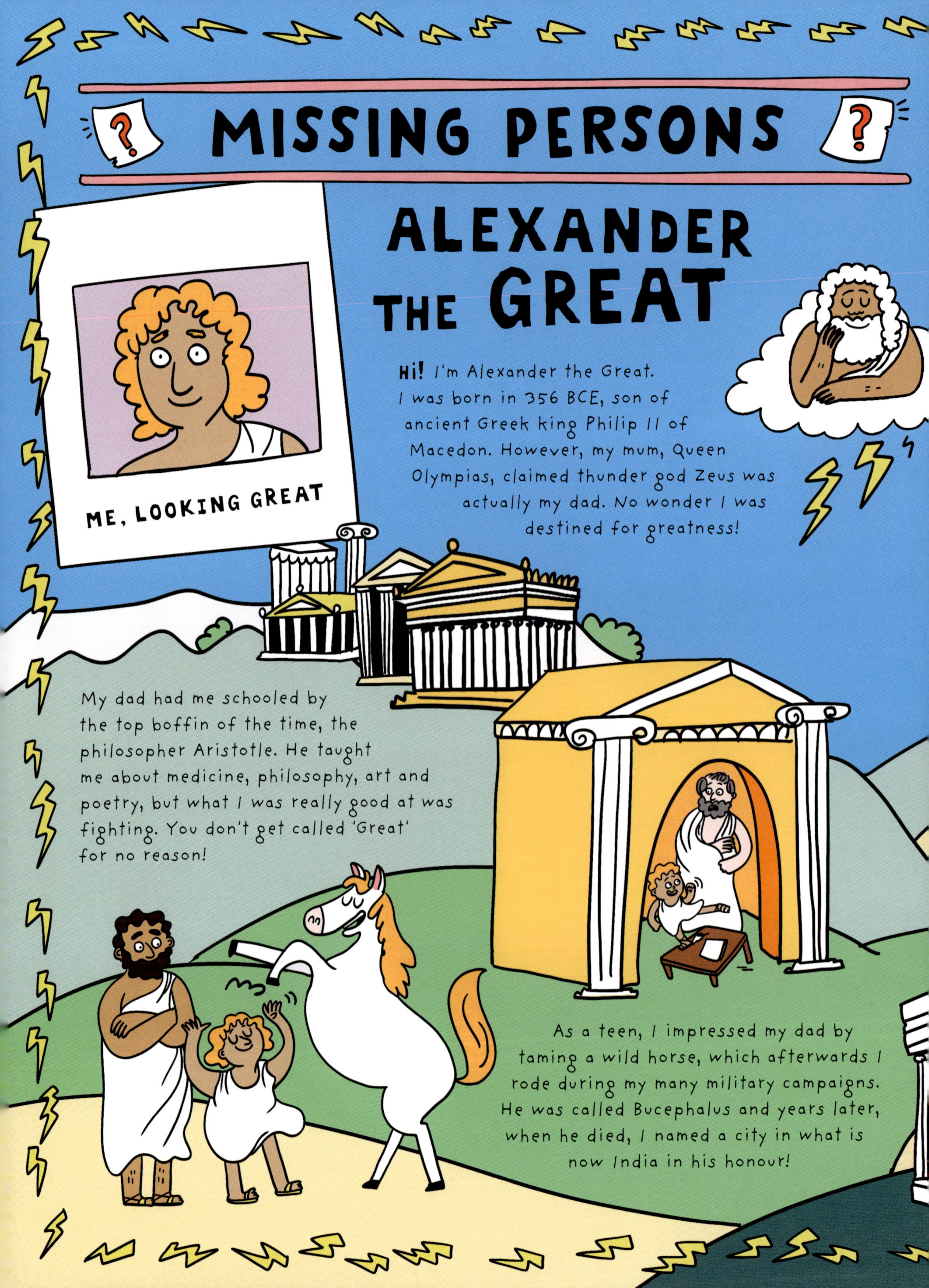

ALEXANDER THE GREAT

Hi! I'm Alexander the Great. I was born in 356 BCE, son of ancient Greek king Philip II of Macedon. However, my mum, Queen Olympias, claimed thunder god Zeus was actually my dad. No wonder I was destined for greatness!

My dad had me schooled by the top boffin of the time, the philosopher Aristotle. He taught me about medicine, philosophy, art and poetry, but what I was really good at was fighting. You don't get called 'Great' for no reason!

As a teen, I impressed my dad by taming a wild horse, which afterwards I rode during my many military campaigns. He was called Bucephalus and years later, when he died, I named a city in what is now India in his honour!

I became king aged 20, when my dad was murdered by his own bodyguard! I'd helped dad win lots of battles by then, and I set out to conquer as many lands as possible. In fact, in 20 battles over 15 years, I never lost one. I was truly Great!

My empire ending up stretching from Greece to northern India, as I attacked towns and cities, killing the men and making slaves of the women and children. Oh, and I usually stole their treasures and sent them home too. It was great being Great!

In 323 BCE, I was in Babylon with king Nebuchadnezzar II (see page 10) when I suddenly became ill and died. I was only 32! My body was placed in a gold coffin and honey added to preserve it. I never lost a battle but still came to a sticky end!

My remains ended up in a temple in Alexandria, Egypt — a city I built and named after myself. Many famous people paid a visit, including Queen Cleopatra, but no one in your time has yet discovered where it stood. That's not great, is it?!

MAUSOLEUM

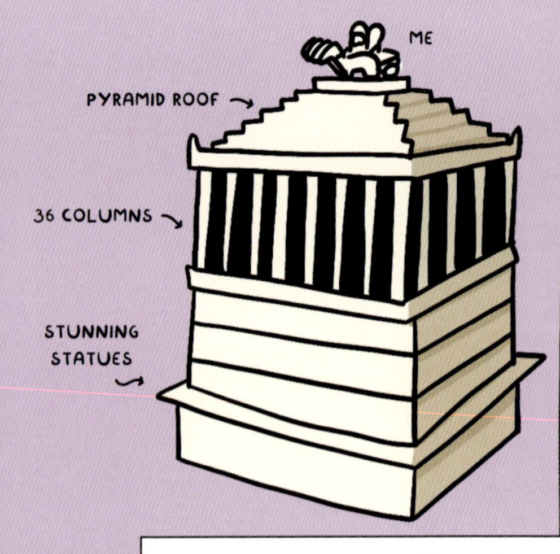
ALONG WITH FELLOW ARCHITECT, SATYROS, THEY DESIGNED THIS MASSIVE MARBLE TOMB AT HALICARNASSUS*...
ME
PYRAMID ROOF →
36 COLUMNS →
STUNNING STATUES
*NOW BODRUM IN MODERN-DAY TURKIYE.

HI! HERE'S A STORY FOR YOU – STRAIGHT FROM THE HORSE'S CARVED MARBLE MOUTH...

I WAS SCULPTED AROUND 350 BCE BY TOP ARCHITECT, PYTHIUS OF PRIENE...
I'M GREEK AND GREAT!

OVER 40 METRES HIGH, IT WAS BUILT FOR A KING CALLED MAUSOLUS...
I'M DYING TO BE IN THERE.

EACH SIDE OF THE MONUMENT WAS THE WORK OF ONE OF THE FOUR GREATEST GREEK SCULPTORS AT THE TIME...
EAST SIDE!
NORTH SIDE!
SOUTH SIDE!
HEY! WE SHOULD FORM A BOY BAND!
SCOPAS
BRYAXIS
TIMOTHEUS
LEOCHARES

CARVINGS INCLUDED CENTAURS – HALF-HUMANS WITH THE LOWER BODIES OF HORSES...
DID WE ACTUALLY EXIST?
NEIGH!

MAUSOLUS DIED IN 353 BCE, LEAVING HIS QUEEN* ARTEMISIA II IN CHARGE...
I'LL FINISH THIS IF IT KILLS ME!
*ALSO HIS SISTER. YUK!

IT DID! SHE DIED TWO YEARS LATER, AND THEIR ASHES WERE PLACED INSIDE.
TOGETHER!
FOREVER!

ON THE VERY TOP WAS A MARBLE CHARIOT WITH FOUR HORSES AND STATUES OF THE KING AND QUEEN...
IT'S A TOMB WITH A VIEW.

SADLY, AN EARTHQUAKE TOPPLED THE TOMB IN THE MIDDLE AGES AND MOST OF IT DISAPPEARED.
FALL!
EEK!
MY HEAD ENDED UP IN A MUSEUM ABROAD.

BUT THE TOMB WAS SUCH A WONDER, IT GAVE THE WORLD THE WORD 'MAUSOLEUM' FOR A BURIAL PLACE.
YES!
TCH! WHY NOT ARTEMISEUM?

TOMB TIME

TOP COPY

Descriptions of the Mausoleum at Halicarnassus have inspired later architects to copy it. Finished in 1930, the Civil Courts Building in St. Louis, in the US state of Missouri, is essentially a small skyscraper with the Mausoleum plopped on top!

TOP TOMB

Now almost 400 years old, the Taj Mahal in Agra, India, was built by Mughal emperor Shah Jahan as a tomb for the body of his beloved wife Mumtaz Mahal. In 2007, it was the winner of a vote to pick the New Seven Wonders of the World.

HARD GUARDS

The world's largest tomb for a known person was built for Qin Shi Huang, the first emperor of China, back in 210 BCE. The size of a city, his giant mausoleum was guarded by 8,000 life-size clay models of soldiers, known as the Terracotta Warriors.

FINAL FANTASY

In Ghana, Africa, deceased people rest in brilliantly colourful 'fantasy coffins' that reflect the career or interests of the occupants when alive. Cleverly constructed by skilled carpenters, many (empty) coffins are now displayed in museums worldwide.

LIGHTHOUSE OF ALEXANDRIA

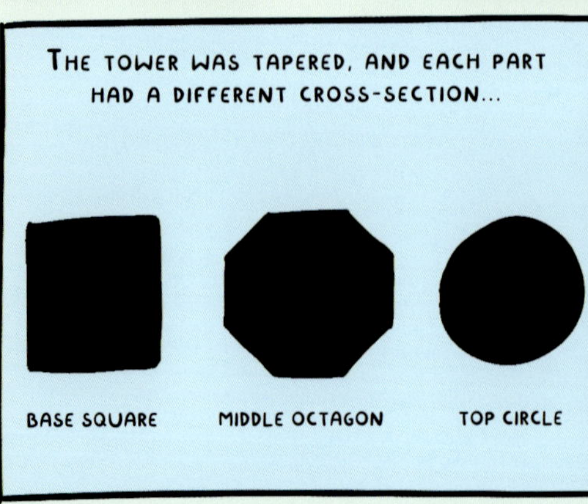

SOME REMAINS WERE REDISCOVERED IN THE HARBOUR IN THE 1990S.

TOWER RECORDS

TALL ORDER

Today's tallest building is the Burj Khalifa skyscraper in Dubai, United Arab Emirates, at almost 828 metres tall. However, when it is finally finished, the Jeddah Tower in Saudi Arabia will then be crowned king at over 1 kilometre high.

WHAT AN EYEFUL

One of the world's best-loved landmarks, the Eiffel Tower in Paris, France, spent a little over 40 years as the world's tallest building, beginning in 1889. It was meant to be taken down just 20 years later, but it was saved by being used as a radio signals transmitter.

SMALL WONDER

The Lighthouse of Alexandria wasn't added to the list of ancient wonders until the sixth century CE. Amazingly, what is thought to be a small copy just 20 metres high, but almost as old, still stands at the nearby coastal town of Abusir, Egypt.

HIGH CHURCH

When its new 160-metre-high spire was built in 1311 CE, Lincoln Cathedral, in the east of England, had a run of several hundred years as the world's tallest building. It took the title from the only ancient wonder still standing today.

Find out which over the page!

GREAT PYRAMID

The Great Pyramid of Giza, on the outskirts of the modern-day Egyptian capital of Cairo, was built as a tomb for Pharaoh Khufu (also called Cheops) over 2,500 years ago. It's the only remaining ancient wonder. Here are some great points about the pyramid!

Over 146 metres high when finished, it was the **world's tallest building** for 3,800 years!

The pyramid was built so that each side exactly faces one of the **four points of the compass** – north, south, east and west!

It was originally covered with **white limestone slabs** that made it shine in the sun, but most of it was removed to use on other building works.

Built by an army of skilled workers, over **2 million** blocks of stone were used – some weighing as much as two adult elephants!

Close by the pyramid is the **Great Sphinx** – a huge stone sculpture with a human head and a lion's body. Its nose has been missing for many centuries!

CHAPTER 2
LOST LEADERS

Kings and queens rule, okay? That's their job, of course, and throughout the ages some have done it better than others. In this chapter, we check out some monster monarchs who were once mighty rulers, but are now simply history. But first, four right royal facts!

MOST MYTHICAL MONARCH

Legendary English King Arthur was invented by writers in the Middle Ages. In 1191, monks at Glastonbury Abbey, England, claimed to have found his grave — maybe as a stunt to attract visitors!

OLDEST PASSPORT HOLDER

The 3,000 year old mummy of ancient Egyptian pharaoh Ramses II was flown to France in 1976 along with a passport that said, 'Profession: King (deceased)'.

ITCHIEST TRIGGER FINGER

Seventeenth century Queen Christina of Sweden supposedly kept a tiny crossbow beside her bed to shoot some of her smallest and most irritating subjects, fleas.

ICE MAIDEN

In 1740, Russian empress Anna Ivanovna built an entire palace and everything in it — including a giant bed — from carved blocks of ice and made her court jester sleep in it.

CLEOPATRA

HELLO. I'M A POISONOUS SNAKE CALLED AN ASP.
LET ME TELL YOU ABOUT ANCIENT EGYPTIAN QUEEN CLEOPATRA VII THEA PHILOPATOR...
CLEO FOR SHORT.

CLEO REIGNED FROM 51 TO 30 BCE BUT IS STILL CELEBRATED OVER 2,000 YEARS ON.
I'M EGYPT'S FANTASTICALLY FAMOUS FEMALE PHARAOH.
AND MODEST WITH IT...

LEGEND HAS IT SHE KILLED HERSELF USING ONE OF MY ANCESTORS.
DID I GRASP AN ASP FOR THIS TERRIBLE TASK? READ ON!
HISS!
CLEO'S LIFE WAS COMPLICATED... FOR A START, SHE WAS ACTUALLY GREEK, BUT SPOKE ANCIENT EGYPTIAN...
YES MA'AM.

SHE BECAME QUEEN AGED 18 BUT HAD TO RULE WITH HER LITTLE BROTHER.
AWKWARD.
TELL ME ABOUT IT.

LATER, HE FORCED HER OUT OF EGYPT. WHILE FIGHTING TO GET BACK HER CROWN, SHE HAD A BABY WITH ROMAN RULER JULIUS CAESAR.
HE HAS HIS FATHER'S LAUREL LEAVES.
GOO!
CAESAR HELPED REMOVE CLEO'S BROTHER, BUT WAS KNIFED TO DEATH BY PLOTTERS IN 44 BCE.
HELP ASSASSINATE CAESAR?
I'LL HAVE A STAB AT IT.

SHE RETURNED TO EGYPT, WHERE ANOTHER BROTHER WAS NOW RULER. BUT CLEO (PROBABLY) HAD HIM POISONED.
HANDY STUFF THIS!

SHE THEN MARRIED AND HAD CHILDREN WITH ANOTHER ROMAN GENERAL, MARK ANTHONY.
THIS IS BECOMING A HABIT...
GOO-GOO!
GOO!
IN 30 BCE, BOTH MARK ANTHONY AND CLEO COMMITTED SUICIDE AFTER LOSING A BATTLE TO A RIVAL ROMAN GENERAL, OCTAVIAN. SHE IS EGYPT'S FINAL PHARAOH.
NO ONE'S TAKING ME PRISONER!

CLEO PROBABLY USED POISON, NOT AN ASP, BUT NO ONE KNOWS WHERE THEY WERE BURIED.
THAT'S HISS-TORY FOR YOU!

PHARAOH STORIES

FACE VALUE

Cleopatra ruled from the Egyptian city of Alexandria. Archaeologist Kathleen Martinez, a Dominican fan of the pharaoh, has spent years searching for Cleopatra's tomb in a nearby temple dedicated to the god Osiris, unearthing coins with Cleo's head on them.

NEEDLE TIME

Both *New York City* in the USA and London, UK, have ancient Egyptian obelisks — tall needle-shaped columns — that have been nicknamed Cleopatra's Needle. They were each found in Alexandria, but are far older than the time of her reign.

DONKEY WORK

To keep her skin soft, Cleo is said to have had a daily bath in warm donkey's milk. It is thought to have needed milk from 700 donkeys to top up her tub, and their milk is still used in some skincare products today!

SMASH HIT

Though we can't yet find Cleopatra on Earth, her precise location on the planet Venus is well known to astronomers. She has a 100-kilometre-wide crater named after her on the planet's surface, caused by the impact of some object from space.

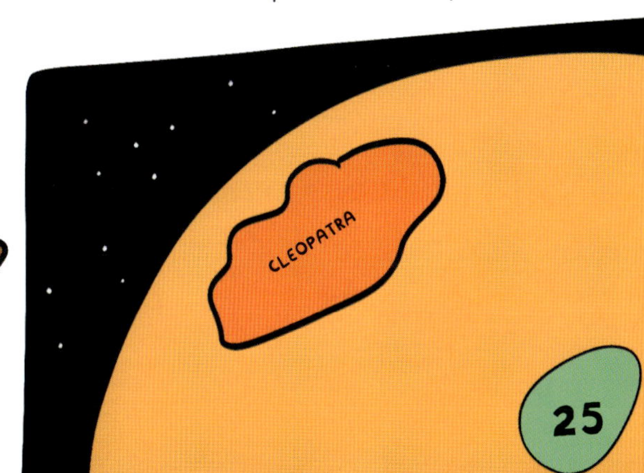

GENGHIS KHAN

Hello. I'm Genghis Khan, the mighty Mongolian emperor. If you don't believe me, I'll take that as a sign of disloyalty and have you killed. I did a lot of killing in my lifetime — as many as 40 million people it's said. The most of any medieval monarch ever!

BIG ME (POSSIBLY)

That picture of me is just a guess. No known portrait of me exists. I was born about 1162 and my Mongol chieftain dad called me Temüjin. Legend has it I came into the world clutching a blood clot in my hand — a sign I would be a great leader.

There were lots of rival tribes living on the vast grassland known as the Mongolian steppe back then, and they were always fighting and killing each other. Indeed, one of them poisoned my dad, leaving me, my mum and brothers struggling to survive.

My bride Borte (possibly)

Well, one of my older half brothers didn't have to struggle for long. I soon killed him in a fight. As a teen I was captured and made a slave by another rival tribe, then I was married, but my bride was then kidnapped. It was a busy childhood!

Long story short, after that I got rival tribes together to form a huge army with me in charge that went all over Asia killing, conquering and looting treasures. That's why in 1206 I renamed myself Genghis Khan — 'Khan' meaning ruler.

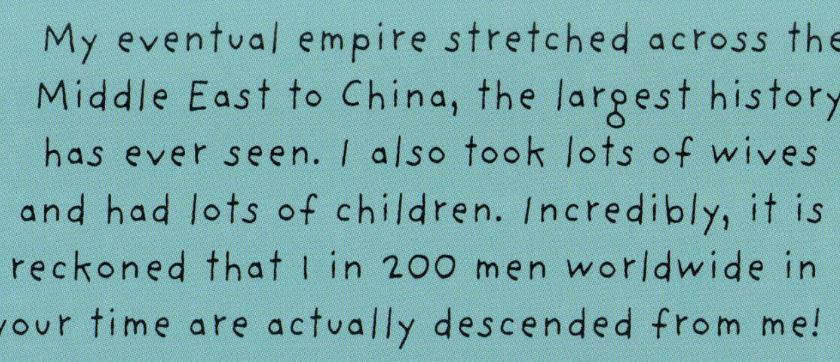

My eventual empire stretched across the Middle East to China, the largest history has ever seen. I also took lots of wives and had lots of children. Incredibly, it is reckoned that 1 in 200 men worldwide in your time are actually descended from me!

Me as khan (possibly)

Me on a horse (possibly)

My final resting place (probably)

I died in 1227 possibly after falling from a horse and was buried on a sacred mountainside at a spot I chose in my youth. Despite my fame, no one knows the exact location, in part because my funeral procession killed everyone they met on the way. Oops!

PUYI

HI! IT'S 1960, AND I'M A BUNCH OF BAMBOO IN THE BEIJING BOTANICAL GARDENS, CHINA...

THIS MAN IS A GARDENER, BUT AS A CHILD HE DIDN'T GROW PLANTS...
TRUE.
WATER!

HE GREW ANGRY! THAT WAS BECAUSE HE WAS PUYI, CHINA'S LAST EVER EMPEROR!
BOW DOWN BEFORE ME OR I SHALL HAVE YOU FLOGGED!
YES, DIVINE ONE.
BEND!

IN 1908, AGED JUST 2, HE WAS DRAGGED TO THE FORBIDDEN CITY PALACE AND MADE EMPEROR AGAINST HIS WISHES.
I WANT MY MUMMY.
SORRY, NOT POSSIBLE.

GROWING UP, SERVANTS DID EVERYTHING FOR HIM – POSSIBLY EVEN COOLING HIS SOUP.
THIS IS A LOW BLOW.
SHUSH, OR I SHALL HAVE YOU FLOGGED.
BLOW!

UTTERLY SPOILED, HE REGULARLY HAD SERVANTS FLOGGED FOR FUN.
SWIPE!
AGAIN!
ANOTHER LOW BLOW. OW!

SECRETLY, HIS SERVANTS GOT REVENGE BY STEALING ROYAL TREASURES AND SELLING THEM.
AND NOW IT'S MY TURN TO FLOG SOMETHING!

A BRITISH TEACHER TAUGHT HIM ENGLISH, AND HE TOOK TO RESTYLING HIS HAIR AND WEARING SPECTACLES.
NOW I WILL SEE THE FLOGGINGS MORE CLEARLY!

HOWEVER, IN 1912, CHINA BECAME A REPUBLIC AND ABOLISHED THE ROLE OF EMPEROR.
WHAT? SOMEONE DESERVES FLOGGING FOR THIS.
ULP!

PUYI ENDED UP AS A PRETEND EMPEROR OF A PART OF CHINA INVADED BY JAPAN...
LUCKILY I STILL GOT TO FLOG PEOPLE!

IN 1945 HE WAS TAKEN PRISONER BY THE SOVIET UNION AND WAS MOCKED FOR NOT KNOWING HOW TO DO BASIC TASKS.
URR, PORRIDGE TOO HOT... BLOW?

THEN IN THE 1950s HE RETURNED TO CHINA AS AN ORDINARY CITIZEN, AND GOT A JOB.
THOSE CANES BRING BACK MEMORIES.

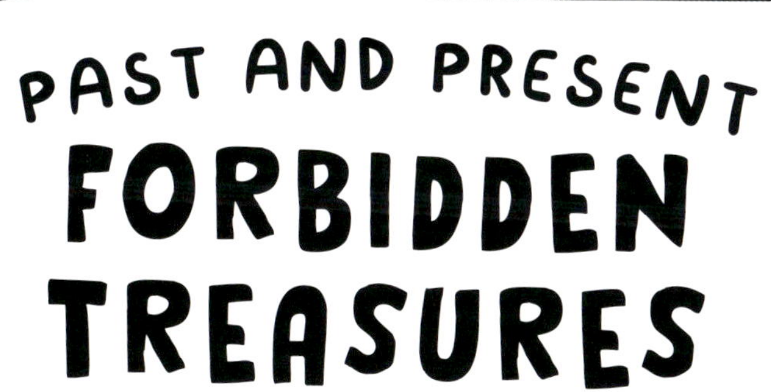

WHAT A SPECTACLE

Puyi died in 1967. His former palace in Beijing is now one of the world's most popular museums with over 17 million visitors per year. Tourists can see his spectacles, golden chopsticks and Imperial seals.

HERE BE DRAGONS!

Many palace buildings have fantastic beasts on their roof, including phoenixes, winged monkeys and dragons. The dragon was the symbol of the power of the emperor and the more beasts on a building, the more important it was.

NO WAY!

The Forbidden City was so-named because it was forbidden for ordinary people to enter. Today, it is open to anyone with a ticket, and they can even pass through the central Meridian Gate, which only the emperor was allowed to use.

CLOCK THIS!

'Zimingzhong' is the charming Chinese word for the palace's display of ornate golden animal-shaped clocks, originally collected by past emperors. They include clocks in the shape of elephants and cranes.

29

CHRYSANTHEMUM THRONE

The world's oldest-surviving monarchy is the Imperial House of Japan. Legend claims it began with Emperor Jimmu, a descendant of the sun goddess, in 660 BCE. More reliably, records trace the actual history back to 539 CE — over 1,400 years ago!

Naruhito is **Japan's 126th emperor** and took on the title in 2019. He is friends with UK King Charles III — though the British royal family goes back only a mere 1,200 years!

Naruhito sat on the ornate takamikura — or **chrysanthemum Throne** — for the emperor-making ceremony. The chrysanthemum flower symbolises the imperial family.

Following Japanese tradition, Naruhito's wife, **Empress Masako,** was given a beautiful rose as a personal symbol when she joined the imperial family.

The **official cars** used by the imperial family are also known as Empresses.

The Imperial Palace in Japan's capital Tokyo has a garden with a different tree representing every district of the nation, including the ginkgo — a tree from before the time of the dinosaurs!

Life began on Earth over 3.5 billion years ago, since then over 99 per cent of its living things, including dinosaurs, have been and gone. Here we unearth some legendary lost life forms and some surprising survivors. But first, four wild facts.

OLDEST INHABITANTS

Shark Bay in Western Australia is peppered with stromatolites — raised rocky columns built by tiny bacteria like those first present at the dawn of life.

LARGEST-EVER INHABITANT

Who needs dinosaurs? At almost 30 metres, the Arctic blue whale is the largest animal known to have existed, yet it feeds on shrimp-like krill the size of a little finger.

GIANT STEPS

Camelotia was a dinosaur that walked on Earth 200 million years ago, leaving footprints that were found on a beach in Wales by 10-year-old Tegan Jones in 2024!

BURNING ISSUE

Coal is a fossilised rock made from plants that grew in forests buzzing with deadly dragonfly-like creatures with wingspans over 70 centimetres, 300 million years ago. Shame to burn it!

THE LAST DINOSAUR

Panel 1:
66 MILLION YEARS AGO, IN WHAT IS NOW ROMANIA, THE LAST DINOSAUR WAS FEEDING...

CHOMP!

MUNCH!

Panel 2:
WELL, IT COMES CLOSE TO LAST IN THE ALPHABET: THE PLANT-EATER **Z**ALMOXES...

KNOW ANY OTHERS THAT BEGIN WITH Z?

Panel 3:
ALSO AROUND WERE SOME EARLY BIRDS AND SMALL FURRY MAMMALS.

FLEE!

DISAPPEAR! THIS STORY IS ALL ABOUT DINOSAURS.

SCAMPER!

JURASSIC PARTS

SAURUS COMING?

Fossils — the preserved remains of long-dead living things — are the best clues to Earth's dinosaur past. In July 2024, a fossilised Stegosaurus known as Apex sold at auction for a staggering $44.6 million US — a record amount for a bunch of stony bones!

DEEPLY DIPPY

Some famous fossils are fakes. Many museums across the world have a 'Dippy' — a 25-metre-long skeleton of a plant-eating Diplodocus from the late Jurassic period. However, the 292 'bones' are actually plaster copies modelled from an original fossil specimen.

ROCK STAR

London's Natural History Museum holds the world's most stupendous stone slab. It depicts Archaeopteryx — a small dinosaur with a beak and feathered wings that helped reveal birds were descended from dinos.

PARK LIFE

'Dinosaurs' didn't actually exist until 1842, when British boffin Sir Richard Owen invented the word. He also designed the first life-size public sculptures of dinosaurs — still on display in a south London park — and a feast was held inside one of them!

WOOLLY MAMMOTH

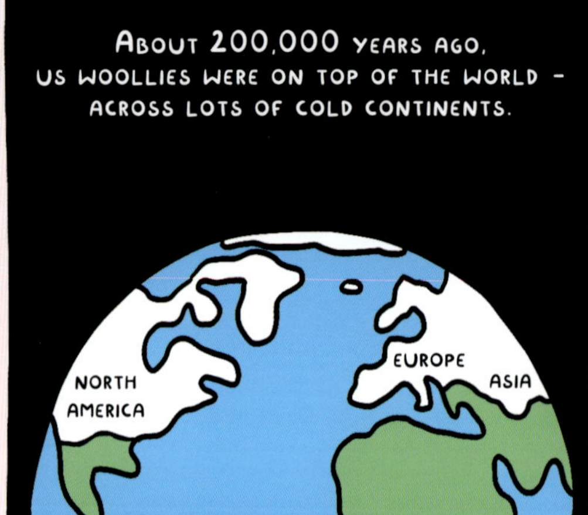

TUSK FORCE

LION THING

One of the world's oldest-known statues is a sculpture carved from mammoth tusk ivory, about 40,000 years ago. The 31-centimetre-high figure with the head of a lion was found in a cave in Germany. When it was made, large European lions were one of mammoths' main threats.

BIG BABY

Being buried in permanently frozen ground has preserved many mammoths. One of the best specimens is Lyuba, a female calf who died about 42,000 years ago. She was found in northern Russia by a reindeer herder who believed touching her would bring bad luck.

HORROR STOREY

Our ancient ancestors didn't just eat mammoths and wear their fur. The collapsed remains of a 12-metre-wide circular hut discovered at Kostenki, Russia, in 2014 was built with the giant bones of at least 60 slaughtered mammoths, 25,000 years ago.

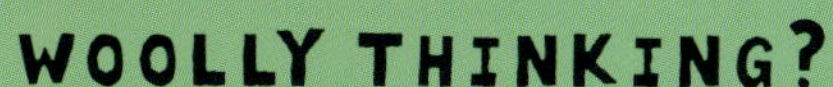

WOOLLY THINKING?

The Asian elephant is the mammoth's closest modern relative, and an American science company reckons it can produce a hairy elephant-mammoth hybrid from preserved mammoth remains. Many, however, can't see the point and say we should focus instead on saving our existing endangered Indian elephants.

NEANDERTHALS

HOMO NEANDERTHALENSIS

Hi! We're Neanderthals, a species of humans different to yours, which lived in small groups across Europe and Asia over 50,000 years ago. My family have asked me to speak for them — though no one is quite sure whether we could talk or not!

Many of us sheltered in caves close to forests. We knew how to use fire, so it could be quite cosy in a cave, though sometimes we had to fight off others for it. Not people — I mean scary lions, bears and hyenas. Eek!

You modern humans once depicted us as primitive, ape-like people, wielding clubs. True, we were stockier than you, with sloping foreheads and big, broad noses — but they helped warm up the cold air before it hit our lungs! It could be chilly back then!

Oh, and while I remember, fossils show our skulls and brains were actually bigger than yours. However, we did miss something you modern humans have — a pointy chin. We were chinless wonders!

Not like this!

More like this!

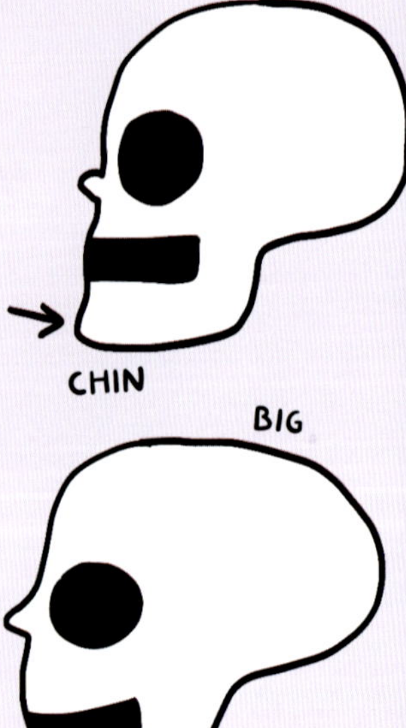

UG UG* (*ME AGAIN)

We had spears and hunted red deer and rabbits in the woods. Meat was a main part of the menu, but Neanderthals near the sea ate fish and seals, while others were vegetarians. Personally, I liked the biggest meaty meal you could get: mammoth!

We also made stone tools and jewellery, cared for our old and injured, and used plants as medicine. Some of us wore animal fur ponchos for warmth, while others went naked in sunnier places. (Maybe I shouldn't have told you that!)

And then about 40,000 years ago, we vanished. Modern humans don't know why, but your ancestors eventually outnumbered us. Some had babies with us, and a small amount of modern human DNA is Neanderthal in origin. We're not totally gone — we live on a little in you! Do you miss us?!

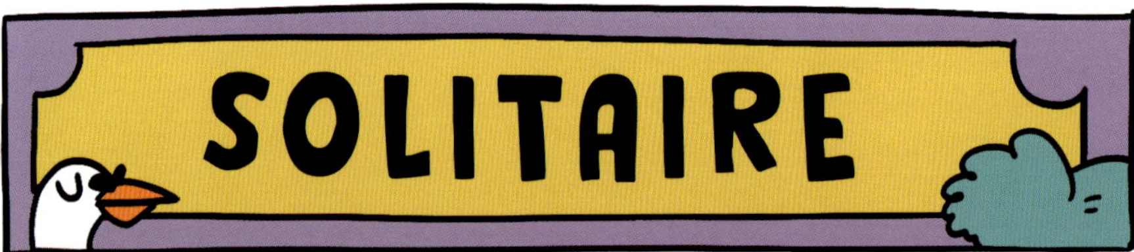

SOLITAIRE

DODOS WERE OUR CLOSEST COUSINS — THOUGH WE ACTUALLY LIVED ON SEPARATE ISLANDS IN THE INDIAN OCEAN, 600 KILOMETRES APART.
NOT THAT CLOSE, REALLY!
CAN'T HEAR YOU!
MAURITIUS (DODOS)
RODRIGUES ISLAND (SOLITAIRES)

HI, I'M LARGE FLIGHTLESS BIRD CALLED A SOLITAIRE.
BECAUSE WE LIKED TO LIVE ALONE.

THIS LARGE FLIGHTLESS BIRD IS MUCH MORE FAMOUS.
YO, I'M A DODO.

DODOS LIVED HAPPILY ON MAURITIUS, EATING FRUITS AND BERRIES, UNTIL HUMANS ARRIVED IN 1598.
HI!
WELL, WE WERE HAPPY...

THEY ALSO BROUGHT ANIMALS THAT ATTACKED THE DODOS AND THEIR EGGS AND CHICKS.
WOOF!
MIAOW!
SQUEAK!
OINK!
NOISY TOO!

JUST OVER 60 YEARS LATER, THE LAST DODO DIED.
FROM DODO TO DEAD-O. URK!

IN 1691, MORE HUMANS LANDED ON OUR OWN ISLAND, RODRIGUES...
HI!
I'M A SOLITAIRE — LEAVE US ALONE.

SADLY, THEY HAD COMPANY TOO...
WOOF!
MIAOW!
SQUEAK!
OINK!
TOO NOISY!

THE HUMANS CUT DOWN THE FORESTS WE LOVED...
THIS TREE IS DEFINITELY FOR THE CHOP.

US BIRDS ALSO GOT THE CHOP...
ROAST SOLITAIRE?
JUST THE ONE.

BY SOME TIME AROUND 1760, ALL US SOLITAIRES WERE GONE.
SEEMS A BIT LONELY WITHOUT THEM — AND THE TREES.

SO WHY IS THE DODO BETTER KNOWN FOR BEING EXTINCT THAN THE SOLITAIRE?
SIMPLE. WE'RE DEAD FAMOUS.
PFFT!

FEATHER REPORT

NATURAL WONDER

A museum in Oxford, UK, has the world's only dodo head with skin on it. The specimen inspired Victorian author Lewis Carroll to include a dodo in his 1865 story *Alice in Wonderland*, bringing the bird back to life!

STAR TURN

The solitaire had a constellation in the night sky named after it in 1776. The same star pattern was then later renamed Noctua, The Owl. Today, the stars are part of the sea snake constellation, Hydra.

WINGING IT

The closest-living relative of both the dodo and solitaire is the Nicobar pigeon, found in flocks in countries in the Western Pacific and Southeast Asia. Unlike them, it can fly, which is probably why it has survived.

BONE IDOL

A bird skeleton made from the bones of several different dodos sold at auction for over £340,000 in 2016. It had belonged to a dodo fan who realised he had collected enough separate bones over 40 years to build an almost-complete bird.

STILL WITH US

JUST HIDING!

Two hundred years ago, some scientists couldn't imagine entire species, such as mammoths, could all disappear. They thought they were simply hiding instead! Here are some living things that were thought lost, but luckily have now reappeared.

The **coelacanth** is a fish thought to have died out with the dinosaurs. It was found swimming off the coast of South Africa in 1938.

The **dawn redwood** is a fir tree known only from fossils until it was found alive and well in China in the 1940s. Now it has been planted in parks across the planet.

The **Judean date palm** was brought back to life from a 2,000-year-old seed found by archaeologists in a jar in the ruins of the palace of Herod the Great, a king in ancient Roman times.

The **Laotian rock rat**, found in the Asian country of Laos in 2005, may be the last surviving example of a rare rodent last seen in fossils from 11 million years ago.

Wallace's giant bee is just that. Females are almost 4 centimetres long, with giant jaws to match. Thought to be extinct, one was caught on an Indonesian island in 2019.

CHAPTER 4
BEEN AND GONE

Ever since our species arose in Africa, humans have been going places. First it was on foot, now we fly, drive, ride and slide. In this chapter, we take a tour though vanished vehicles and lost forms of transport, hitting the road with four fab facts!

OLDEST-KNOWN SKIS

Missing for 1,300 years, a wooden ski dating to before the time of the Vikings was found buried in ice in Digervarden, Norway in 2014. Its pair then turned up nearby in 2021!

OLDEST SET OF WHEELS

A pot found in Poland dating back about 5,500 years is decorated with what seems to be a four-wheeled farm wagon.

FIRST AIRBORNE SHEEP

The first animals to fly in a hot-air balloon were a rooster, a duck and a sheep called 'Montauciel'. Lifting off from near Paris, France, in September 1783, they all landed safely!

FURTHEST VEHICLE

The Voyager I space probe was launched in 1977 by US space agency NASA and is now over 25 billion kilometres from Earth — the most distant human-made object ever.

STEAMSHIP

THIS SCENE IS UNTHINKABLE!
THEY SAID SHE WAS UNSINKABLE.
WE'RE ICEBERGS - FLOATING MOUNTAINS OF FROZEN WATER, BUT WE'RE NOT COLD-HEARTED...
NO...
WE WOULD NEVER HAVE WANTED THE ROYAL MAIL SHIP TITANIC TO HIT ONE OF US AND GO DOWN WITH THE LOSS OF OVER 1,500 LIVES IN 1912.

BUILT IN BELFAST, IRELAND, RMS TITANIC WAS A 269-METRE-LONG LUXURY MARITIME MARVEL...
THE LARGEST HUMAN-MADE MOVING OBJECT SO FAR!
WAVE!
TOOT!
COMPLETE WITH A SWIMMING POOL, SQUASH COURT AND GYM!
WAVE!
SHE CAN CARRY OVER 3,000 PASSENGERS AND CREW!

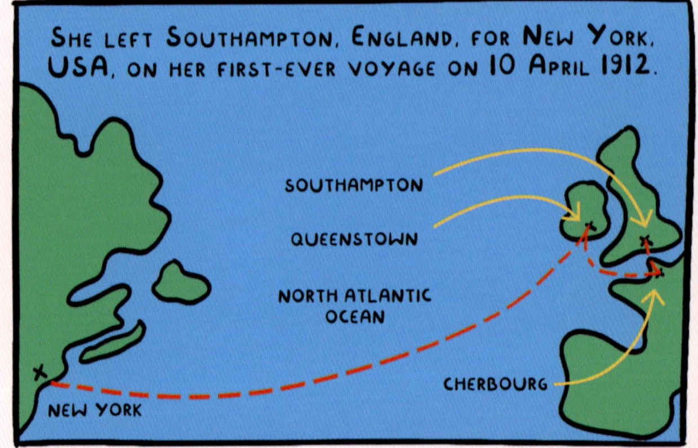

SHE LEFT SOUTHAMPTON, ENGLAND, FOR NEW YORK, USA, ON HER FIRST-EVER VOYAGE ON 10 APRIL 1912.
SOUTHAMPTON
QUEENSTOWN
NORTH ATLANTIC OCEAN
CHERBOURG
NEW YORK

BUT ON THE MOONLESS NIGHT OF 14 APRIL, IN THE ICY NORTH ATLANTIC OCEAN, SHE HIT A PROBLEM...
SCREEK!
ME. SORRY...

HOLED BENEATH THE WATERLINE AND SINKING FAST, THERE WAS ANOTHER PROBLEM...
CAPTAIN SMITH, WE ONLY HAVE LIFEBOAT SPACES FOR ABOUT 1,000 PEOPLE.
AND THERE'S 2,200 ON BOARD. ULP!

THE SHIP SANK IN UNDER THREE HOURS, SPLITTING IN HALF AND HITTING THE SEA BED 3.8 KILOMETRES BELOW. A TRAGEDY OF TRULY TITANIC PROPORTIONS.
GONE!

THE WRECK WAS FINALLY FOUND IN 1985, BUT MAYBE IT SHOULD HAVE BEEN LEFT ALONE?
WE THINK SO.

DEEP DIVE

RUST IN PEACE

You need a super-strong submarine to reach the remains of the Titanic, but hurry! Its metal parts are slowly being eaten by bacteria that produce strands known as 'rusticles' — a mix of the words 'rust' and 'icicle'.

YOUNG AND OLD

Just two months old, British baby Millvina Dean was the youngest passenger on Titanic's doomed voyage and was adored by adults on board. Aged 97, she also lived to be its last-ever survivor, having lost her own father in the tragedy.

HORROR-SCOPE

Futility was a short novel by US author Morgan Robertson. Published in 1898, it was about a giant British luxury liner that hit an iceberg and sank with many lives lost due to too few lifeboats. The name of this ship? The *Titan*. Coincidence?

FULL STEAM AGAIN?

Back in 2012, an Australian billionaire announced a plan to make a modern copy of the ill-fated ship, to be called Titanic II. If it does ever get built, modern shipping laws will make sure it has more than enough lifeboats for everyone.

AIRSHIP

HI. WE'RE ATOMS OF HYDROGEN GAS, THE LIGHTEST ELEMENT IN THE UNIVERSE.

IN 1783, FRENCHMAN JACQUES CHARLES AND A COLLEAGUE FLEW A HYDROGEN-FILLED BALLOON, 40 KILOMETRES FROM PARIS.
WE'VE INVENTED THE AIRSHIP!
WHAT A GAS!

I CALL IT A DIRIGIBLE.
I CALL IT INCREDIBLE!
THE FIRST STEERABLE STEAM-POWERED AIRSHIP WAS ALSO BUILT IN FRANCE, BY HENRI GIFFARD IN 1852.

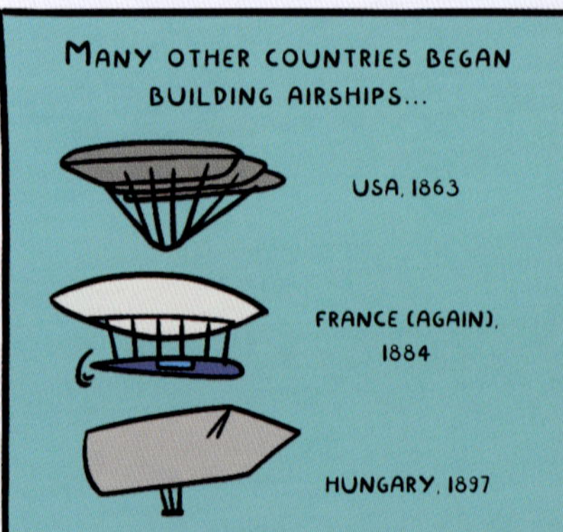

MANY OTHER COUNTRIES BEGAN BUILDING AIRSHIPS...
USA, 1863
FRANCE (AGAIN), 1884
HUNGARY, 1897

AND IN 1900, FORMER GERMAN GENERAL COUNT FERDINAND VON ZEPPELIN BUILT HIS OWN FIRST AIRSHIP, THE LUFTSCHIFF ZEPPELIN 1...
LZ1, FOR SHORT.
SAVES TIME!

SOON, ZEPPELIN AIRSHIPS FLEW PASSENGERS ACROSS OCEANS FASTER THAN STEAMSHIPS.
HA!
SHOW OFF!

VON ZEPPELIN DIED IN 1917, BUT HIS COMPANY KEPT GOING, BUILDING THE WORLD'S LARGEST-EVER AIRSHIP – THE 245-METRE-LONG LZ129 HINDENBURG IN 1936.
IT'S HUGE!
BUT STILL FLOATS THANKS TO THE HYDROGEN!

HYDROGEN GAS WAS LIGHT AND CHEAP, BUT SADLY IS ALSO VERY DANGEROUS.
OH THE HUMANITY!
6 MAY, NEW JERSEY, USA

THE HINDENBURG ACCIDENT ENDED THE AIRSHIP ERA UNTIL PEOPLE STARTED TO USE HELIUM...
THE HELIUM GAS USED IN PARTY BALLOONS IS EXPENSIVE...
FLOAT!
DRIFT!
BUT DOESN'T EXPLODE!

HEY! I THOUGHT WE DIDN'T EXPLODE!
EEK!
BANG!

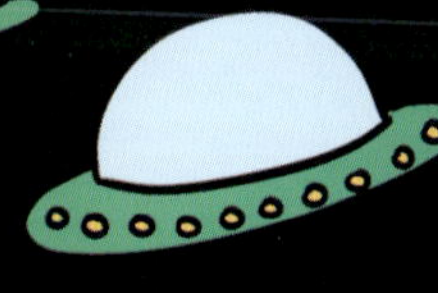

PAST AND PRESENT
BAGS OF FUN

SCARESHIPS

At the end of the 19th century, a wave of people in the USA claimed to have spotted lights in the night sky coming from phantom airships looking like UFOs. After about 150 reports, they stopped suddenly in early 1897...

CLOUD CONTROL

US space agency NASA has proposed exploring the upper atmosphere of the planet Venus using solar-powered airships, with people living in floating cloud cities high above Venus's deadly hot surface.

WHAT A CHEEK!

The Airlander 10 is a modern helium-filled airship that a British company is hoping to use for tourist trips to the North Pole. The airship is nicknamed 'The Flying Bum' — though the 'bum' shape is at the front not the rear!

OUT FOR THE COUNT

French adventurer Stephane Rousson has attempted to cross the English Channel and the Mediterranean Sea slung underneath a small helium-filled airship or 'blimp'. He calls his blimps 'Zeppy', in honour of Count Zeppelin.

AMELIA EARHART

AMELIA EARHART

Hi! I'm Amelia Earhart, and I was born in Kansas, USA, in 1897. My last name is pronounced 'air-heart' — perfect for someone who became one of the most famous aviators of all time! That picture of me is from my pilot's licence!

Growing up, people went to 'air fairs' to watch pilots do tricks, and you also could also fly in a plane yourself. I was only 10 when my dad offered to pay for me to take a trip, but the plane looked so ricketty, I refused. Well, that soon changed!

My interest in flying came from working in a military hospital, helping pilots who had been injured in World War 1. Their stories led to me finally taking a flight at an air fair in 1920. Once I got off the ground, I knew I had to fly!

I had lessons with renowned female flying instructor Neta Snook, working many jobs to pay for them. I also cut my hair short, bought a new leather flying jacket and a second-hand yellow biplane which I nicknamed 'The Canary'.

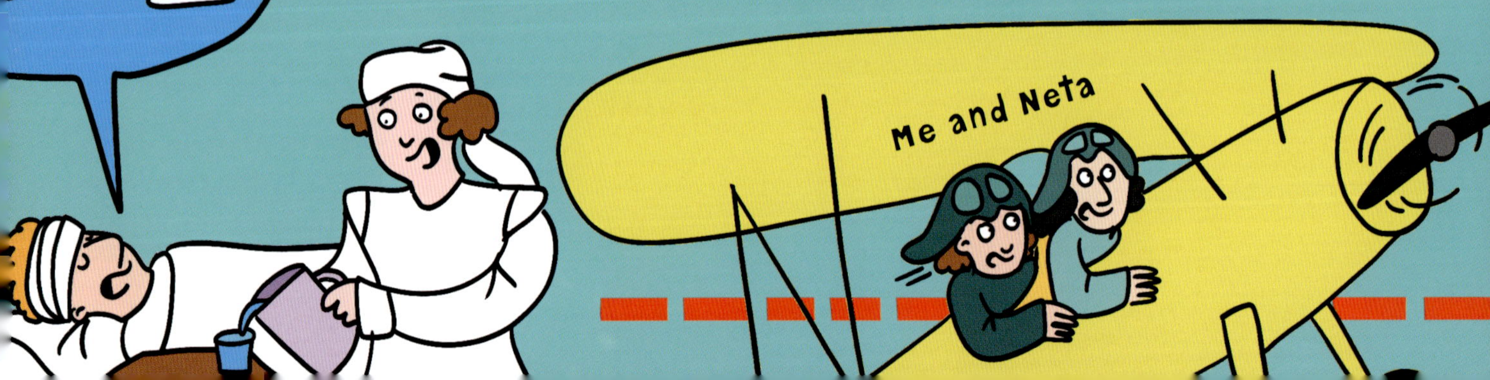

On 22 October 1922, I set a new world record for a female flyer, taking 'The Canary' to a height of 4,300 metres. Little did I know this was to be the first of many records I would set. Even better, in 1923, I was granted my pilot's licence!

In 1928, I became the first woman to fly across the Atlantic Ocean from Canada to the UK. The flight took 20 hours and 40 minutes, and made me world famous, but I was simply a passenger for that. Now, I wanted to pilot the planes myself!

Well, in 1932, I did it! I flew nonstop on my own from Newfoundland, Canada, in a bright red Lockheed 5B Vega, landing in a muddy field in Northern Ireland 15 hours later. Being the first female to fly across the Atlantic alone made me mega-famous and was a powerful symbol of what women could do!

Finally, in 1937, while trying to be the first woman to fly around the world, my plane disappeared. It probably ran out of fuel and crashed into the ocean, but me and my navigator, Fred Noonan, have never been found. It was a sad end for us — and my record-setting attempt!

SUPERSONIC JET

THE JET SET

NOSE FOR A BARGAIN

The drooping nose cone remains the most iconic and collectible part of Concorde. An unused cone sold at auction in 2018 for £63,000 on the nose, so to speak.

GONE IN A FLASH

Only one photo exists of Concorde flying supersonically. The plane had to slow slightly to allow a military jet to take a quick snap before Concorde powered away.

ENGINE ROOM

Sixteen Concordes are on public display in Europe, Barbados and the United States. You can also visit the Museo del Concorde in Chihuahua, Mexico, which exhibits parts from past planes, including a giant Rolls Royce engine.

SO NOISE-SKI!

Nicknamed 'Concordski', the Tupolev Tu-144 was a slightly larger, slightly faster rival to Concorde, built by the Soviet Union. However, engine noise inside the plane was so loud passengers had to shout or write notes to each other.

BOOM TIME

The days of supersonic passenger planes may be soon returning. American company Boom Industries plans to build a fleet of luxury 'Overture' airliners that it hopes will take to the air in 2029.

PLASTIC CAR

DRIVERS SPEAK HIGHLY OF MANY GERMAN MAKES OF CAR...
BMW
AUDI
MERCEDES-BENZ
VW

BUT ONLY ONE GERMAN-MADE CAR LITERALLY TURNED THE AIR BLUE – DUE TO ITS UNRELIABILITY AND SMOKY EXHAUST!
VVVRRRRMMM!

THE TINY TRABANT – 'TRABI', FOR SHORT – WAS MADE IN EAST GERMANY FROM 1957 TO 1991.
100 KILOMETRES PER HOUR 'TOP' SPEED
MOULDED PLASTIC BODY
BEAT YOU!
VVRRRMM!
JUST 3.5 METRES LONG!

AFTER WORLD WAR II, GERMANY WAS SPLIT INTO EAST AND WEST, AND THE BORDER BETWEEN THEM CLOSED...
COME AND SEE US!
WE'RE NOT ALLOWED!
WEST
EAST

IN EAST GERMANY, PEOPLE HAD A SIMPLE CHOICE WHEN IT CAME TO OWNING A CAR...
TRABANT, OR NO TRABANT?
HMM, TRICKY...

THEN THEY WAITED UP TO TEN YEARS FOR DELIVERY.
YOUR CAR IS NOW READY.
AT LAST!

THE NOISY, SMELLY, BADLY BUILT CARS WERE THE BUTT OF MANY JOKES...
HOW DO YOU DOUBLE THE VALUE OF A TRABI?
FILL UP HER FUEL TANK!

BUT THEY BECAME WORLD FAMOUS IN 1989 WHEN THE EAST GERMAN BORDER WAS FINALLY OPENED AND A TRAIL OF TRABIS HEADED WEST!
HURRY! A SNAIL IS TRYING TO OVERTAKE US!
VVRRRMM!

ONCE THERE, MANY WERE DUMPED IN FAVOUR OF FAR BETTER WEST GERMAN CARS.
GOODBYE, SHABBY TRABI.
SOB!
ABANDONED!

TODAY, SURVIVING TRABIS ARE HIGHLY PRIZED COLLECTORS' ITEMS...
I CAN'T WAIT TO OWN ONE.
LUCKILY YOU NO LONGER NEED TO!

FANTASTIC PLASTIC

SHHH!

The International Spy Museum in Washington DC, USA, does actually exist — but, please, don't tell anyone. Since 2006, it has hosted an annual parade of Trabants, including a challenge to visitors to see if they could hide inside one to get past border guards!

WALL FLOWER

The city of Berlin was divided by a concrete wall built by East Germany in 1961 to stop citizens escaping to the West. It began to be demolished in 1989, and a surviving segment has a famous mural by artist Birgit Kinder showing her Trabi bursting through unscathed.

SUPER-COUPE

Invented in 1979 by US car designer Jim Mariol, the 'Cozy Coupe' plastic play car made by the Little Tikes toy company, is consistently one of the world's bestselling vehicles. Jim was inspired by scooting around on an office chair with wheels.

TRABI V STRATI

'Strati' is an electric car made in 2014 by a process known as 3D printing, where parts are formed from layers of heated plastic instructed by a computer. However, with a top speed of just 64 kilometres per hour a surviving Trabi could take it any day. Perhaps.

MUSEUM PIECES

Many of history's most famous vehicles are now safely parked in museums around the world. Indeed, some of those vehicles may have actually travelled around the world themselves. Here is a selection of now-stationary stars!

Vostok 1 is the space capsule in which Soviet Union cosmonaut Yuri Gagarin made the first space-orbit of Earth in 1961. It is on display at a massive museum in Moscow, Russia.

In December 1903, Orville Wright piloted the first sustained flight in a heavier-than-air machine built with his brother Wilbur. Flyer I now rests in a flight museum in Washington DC, USA — as does Amelia Earhart's red **Lockheed 5B Vega**. (See page 47).

Olton Hall is the actual name of the black and red steam locomotive that delivers young wizards to Hogwarts in the Harry Potter films. Built in 1937, it stands in a replica of Platform 9 ¾ in a movie museum just outside London, UK.

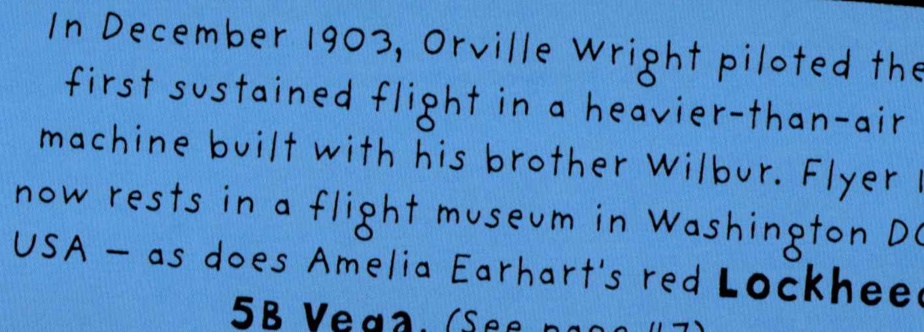

The **Oseberg longship**, a well-preserved Viking sailing vessel, is on display at a museum in Oslo, Norway. Built about 800 CE, a seaworthy modern copy of the ship has been made that allows visitors to go on board and be part of its crew!

The world's **oldest-known wooden wheel** was found outside Slovenian capital Ljubljana in 2002, and can be seen in the city's museum. Made of ash and oak, it has been dated back over 5,000 years.

CHAPTER 5
OUT OF PLACE

It should be a little difficult to lose something as a big as a city, but history has shown us that time, floods, volcanoes and other disasters can bring it about. This chapter looks at places that are literally off the map, beginning with a quick quartet of facts.

LARGEST LOST CITY?

Mohenjo-daro in modern Pakistan was the greatest city of the ancient Indus Valley Civilisation. Lost for over 3,400 years, it was only unearthed in the 1920s.

CLOUDED IN MYSTERY

'Lost' is a tiny village in Aberdeenshire, Scotland. Its unusual name meant its road sign was constantly going missing and having to be replaced.

WELCOME TO NOWHERE

The German city of Bielefield does exist, though an internet hoax started in 1994 by a computer science student insisted it didn't. Ironically, the viral joke put the town on the map!

MAP TRAP

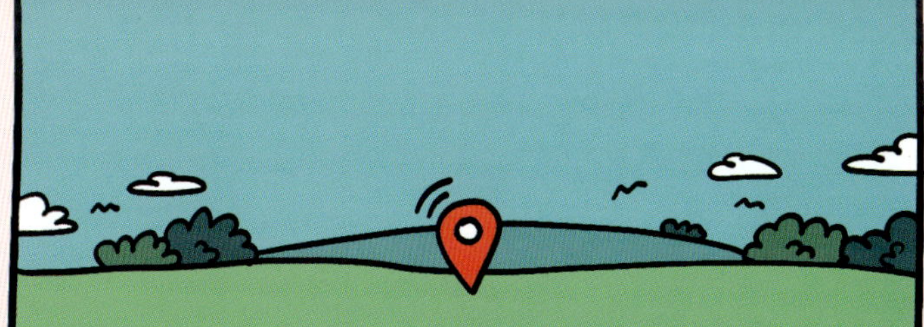

Argleton was a phantom town in north-west England shown on Google maps until 2010. In fact, it was just empty fields and has now been removed.

HERCULANEUM

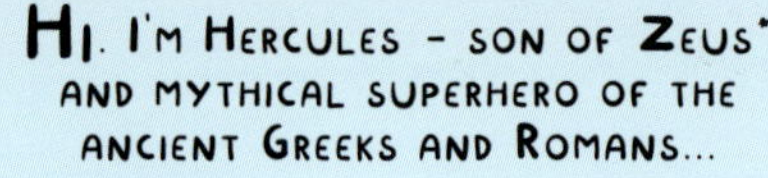

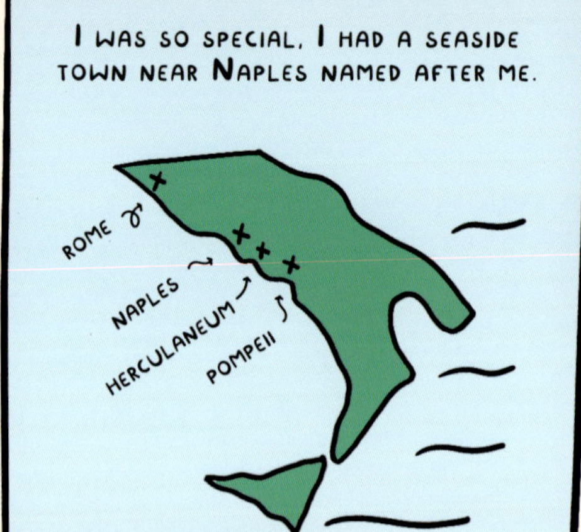

BURIED TREASURES

TOP TOWN

The town on top of the ruins of Herculaneum used to be called Resina. In 1969, residents agreed to rename it Ercolano, a modern Italian version of the original name of the ancient Roman resort.

RAYS OF HOPE

The Villa of the Papyri is the name of a luxury dwelling discovered in 1750. It had a library of 1,800 scrolls made from papyrus – an early form of paper – that scientists still hope to read one day using special X-ray machines.

PIGS MIGHT FRY

The Villa of the Papyri was home to many fine statues of Roman gods, goddesses and other mythological figures. There was also a life-size bronze of a leaping piglet – possibly a symbol of the joy to be found in feasting well.

CALIFORNIA DREAMING

Opened in 1974, The Getty Villa in Los Angeles, USA, is a copy of the Villa of the Papyri built by billionaire businessman J Paul Getty. A museum dedicated to the ancient world, visitors can experience how Herculaneum looked before it was buried alive.

MISSING PERSONS
PERCY FAWCETT
LIEUTENANT COLONEL PERCY HARRISON FAWCETT
Hello! I'm Lieutenant colonel Percy Harrison Fawcett, and I was born in Torquay, southern England, in 1867. I'm rather proud of the moustache I have in that picture of me!
SRI LANKA (CEYLON)
Treasure?
After school, I went to military college and served as spy in Ceylon (known as Sri Lanka today). One day I was told the location of a lost buried treasure. Rushing into the forest, I found only rocks, but the thrill of looking changed my life forever.
My secret assignment
Back in London in 1901, I joined the Royal Geographical Society and proved rather good at making maps. So good that in 1902, I was sent to Morocco to map the land, though I was actually also working as a spy for the British government. Shh!

In 1906, the Society sent me to South America to map the Amazon jungle between Bolivia and Brazil. I encountered flesh-eating piranha fish and a giant anaconda snake that was 19 metres long — but no one at home believed me!

There were many native tribes in the rainforest. I gave them gifts and in return they shared such wonders as the double-nosed tiger hound, which they bred for hunting jaguars. (Again no one believed me!)

'Z'?

After World War I, I returned to South America where I read an old document in a Brazilian library describing a lost city with arches, a temple and gold. I called it 'The Lost City of Z' — and I had to find it! Easier said than done. In 1920, my solo expedition failed.

our last location

In 1925, I tried again, accompanied by my eldest son Jack and his friend Raleigh Rimmel. We set off into the Brazilian jungle... One tribe later said they saw smoke from our campfire for five days, then — nothing. Whatever happened, 'Z' has never been found. And neither have we!

My last letter home ended with the words, 'You need have no fear of failure.' Well, perhaps my biggest failure was to open the way for other explorers to come and trouble the indigenous people. Some lost things are better off staying lost..

PETRA
RAQMU

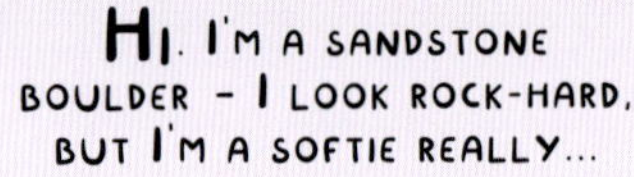

HI. I'M A SANDSTONE BOULDER - I LOOK ROCK-HARD, BUT I'M A SOFTIE REALLY...

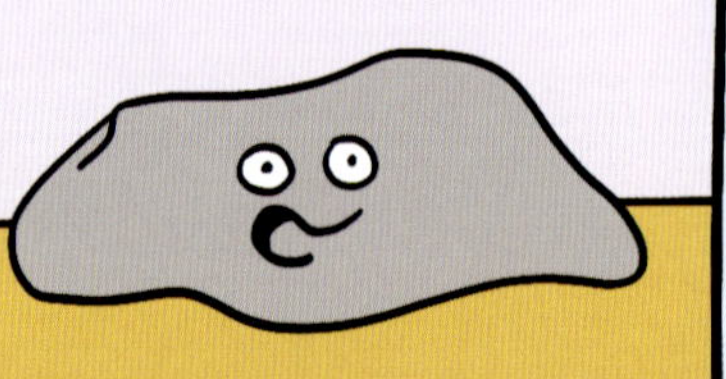

SO SOFT THAT THE ANCIENT PEOPLE OF THE CITY OF PETRA COULD CARVE OUT THESE INCREDIBLE BUILDINGS SOME 2,000 YEARS AGO.
'THE TREASURY'
'THE MONASTERY'
'THE ROYAL TOMB'

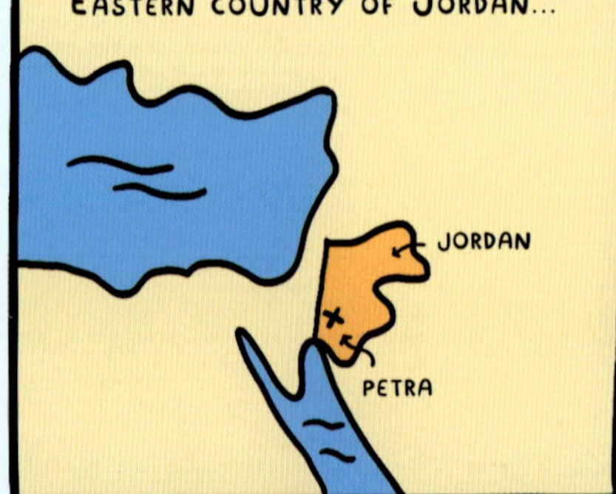

TODAY, PETRA IS IN THE MIDDLE EASTERN COUNTRY OF JORDAN...
JORDAN
PETRA

IT WAS BUILT BY THE NABATAEANS, ANCIENT ARABS NOW LOST TO HISTORY...
WE'RE NOT LOST!
WE'RE IN RAQMU*...
* THE ORIGINAL NAME FOR PETRA.

IT GREW BECAUSE IT WAS AT THE CROSSROADS OF TWO MAJOR TRADING ROUTES.
I WOULDN'T TRADE RAQMU FOR ANYWHERE ELSE!
ME NEITHER!

THE ANCIENT GREEKS CALLED THE CITY 'PETRA' - WHICH MEANS 'ROCK'...
FANCY A GAME OF PETRA, PAPER, SCISSORS?
YOU'RE ON!

THE ROMANS TOOK IT OVER, BUT IT WAS HIT BY AN EARTHQUAKE IN 363 CE.
THIS CITY ROCKS!
LITERALLY... EEK!
RUMBLE!

CRUSADERS CAME IN THE MIDDLE AGES, BUT EVENTUALLY IT BECAME A 'LOST' CITY, KNOWN ONLY TO LOCALS...
WE'RE NOT LOST!
WE'RE IN RAQMU

IN 1812, A SWISS EXPLORER WAS THE FIRST EUROPEAN TO VISIT IN A VERY LONG TIME...
THIS GORGE IS GORGE-OUS!

IN 2007, AN ONLINE POLL NAMED PETRA AS ONE OF THE SEVEN NEW WONDERS OF THE WORLD...
ROCK ON!

AND TODAY, MILLIONS OF VISITORS STAND IN AWE OF ITS RUINS...
YOU OKAY?
I'M PETRA-FIED!

NEW WONDERS

BIG HITTER

Completed in 1931, Christ the Redeemer is the newest of the *New Seven Wonders*. Standing 30 metres tall on a peak overlooking Rio de Janeiro, Brazil, the iconic statue gets struck occasionally by lightning!

LOST AND FOUND

Many people's idea of a 'lost city', the Inca mountain fortress of Machu Picchu in Peru was not widely known until the early 20th century. It is over 500 years old.

HIGHER MAYA

Chichén Itzá, Mexico, was a city built by the Mayan people over 800 years ago. Its largest pyramid, El Castillo, is 30 metres tall and topped with a temple.

DARK DOUBLE

India's white marble tomb, the Taj Mahal (see page 19), could have had an opposite. Emperor Shah Jahan planned to build a twin in black marble, but it got cancelled.

COLOSSAL SIZE

Rome's Colosseum is the largest ancient amphitheatre ever built. Finished in 80 CE, it staged gladiator fights as well as cruel animal hunts and human executions.

WONDER WALL

The oldest of the 'Seven New Wonders', China's Great Wall has parts dating back over 2,700 years. To stop insects attacking it, the deadly poison arsenic was added during building, making it a Wonder you really can't lick!

MARS

HI. I'M EARTH'S NEAREST NEIGHBOUR, MARS.
ALSO KNOWN AS 'THE RED PLANET'.

IN THE YEAR 1877, TOP ITALIAN ASTRONOMER GIOVANNI SCHIAPARELLI THINKS HE SEES CHANNELS ON MY SURFACE.
I CALL THEM 'CANALI'.

JUST BARGE-ING ABOUT.
ME TOO.
WELL, THIS GETS MISTRANSLATED INTO ENGLISH AS 'CANALS', LIKE THE ONES BOATS AND SHIPS USE ON EARTH.

ENTER US ASTRONOMER PERCIVAL LOWELL (JUST OVER 100 YEARS AGO)
OBSERVE, I HAVE AN OBSERVATORY!

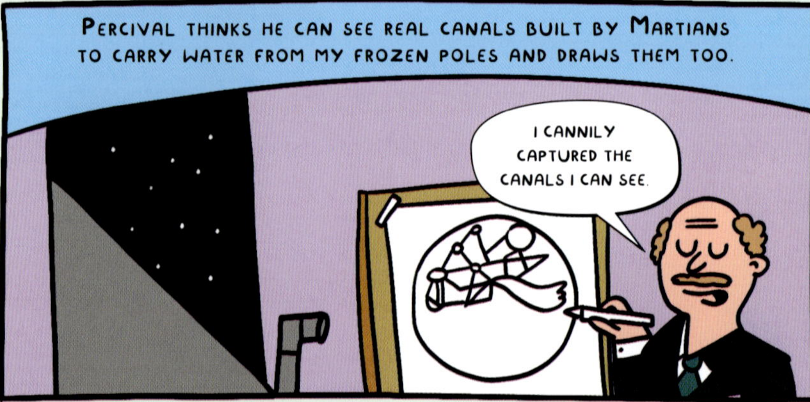

PERCIVAL THINKS HE CAN SEE REAL CANALS BUILT BY MARTIANS TO CARRY WATER FROM MY FROZEN POLES AND DRAWS THEM TOO.
I CANNILY CAPTURED THE CANALS I CAN SEE.

HE ALSO PUBLISHES BOOKS ABOUT THE IDEA...
MARS and its CANALS
MARS as the ABODE of LIFE
1906
1908

ALL THIS MAKES THE PUBLIC THINK I ONCE HAD MARTIANS CAPABLE OF CREATING CANALS.
DIG!
SHOVEL!

AND THEY PROBABLY LIVED IN MANY MARTIAN CITIES.
TWINNED WITH SATURNOPOLIS

PLENTY OF EXPERTS ARGUED AGAINST LIFE ON MARS...
TOO COLD.
TOO DRY.
TOO MUCH DIGGING.

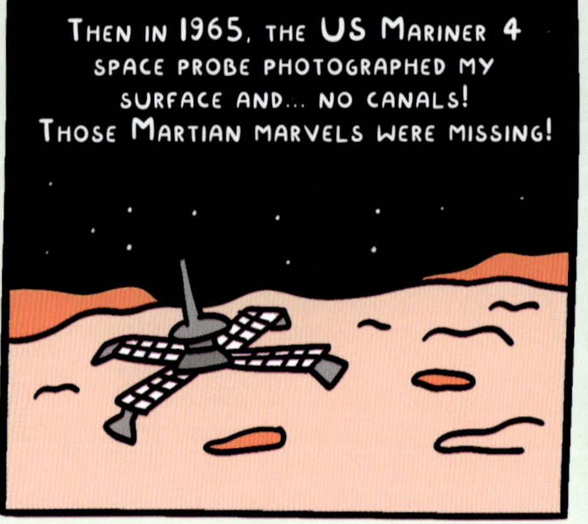

THEN IN 1965, THE US MARINER 4 SPACE PROBE PHOTOGRAPHED MY SURFACE AND... NO CANALS! THOSE MARTIAN MARVELS WERE MISSING!

AND NO SIGNS OF LIFE EITHER...
JUST CALL ME 'THE DEAD PLANET'.

LOCK AND QUAY

WATER STAR

Passing through China's capital Beijing, its Grand Canal ticks two boxes when it comes to records. Built in the 5th century BCE, it is both the world's oldest surviving canal and its longest human-made waterway at 1,794 kilometres.

MOVE IT!

In 2021, a 400-metre-long container ship called the *Ever Given* ran aground and blocked Egypt's Suez Canal for six days before being tugged free. The stuck ship became famous as an internet meme for people's problems.

MARS BAR

Ambitious Earthlings have already drawn up plans to build cities on Mars, though a supply of water would be needed to live there. It may exist in the form of ice at the planet's frozen poles or hidden under the ground.

PAINT IT BLACK

Venice's Grand Canal is just 3.8 kilometres long, but famous with it. The Italian city's waterborne taxis are called gondolas and a 500 year old city law says they all have to be painted black!

STILL WITH US

OLDEST RESIDENTS

Humans have been choosing to gather together — then moan about their neighbours — for thousands of years. Here are the oldest continuously inhabited places on each of Earth's contents.

EUROPE

Plovdiv, Bulgaria, has evidence of stone age settlements dating back about 8,000 years.

ASIA

Syria is home to Damascus — the world's oldest continuously inhabited capital city — and Aleppo, where finds have been dated back over 11,000 years.

AUSTRALASIA

Evidence suggests that Aboriginal people lived around Sydney, Australia, more than 30,000 years ago.

NORTH AMERICA

People have lived in Cholula, a district of Puebla, Mexico, for about 3,000 years — right next to their Great Pyramid neighbour (see page 9).

AFRICA

Girga in Egypt has been occupied for over 6,000 years and may have been the base for the first ever pharaoh, Narmer.

SOUTH AMERICA

Quito, Ecuador, has been lived in since 980 CE, but its origins may go back another 3,000 years!

ANTARCTICA

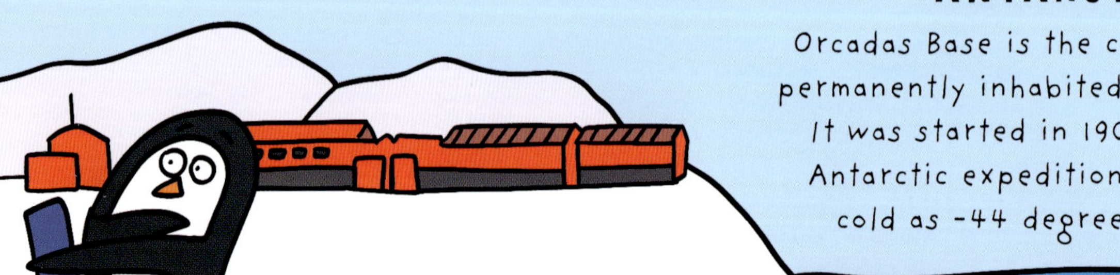

Orcadas Base is the continent's oldest permanently inhabited research station. It was started in 1903 by a Scottish Antarctic expedition and can fall as cold as -44 degrees Celsius. Brr!

CHAPTER 6
LOST PROPERTIES

Modern cities all have buildings that come and go, while others may become lasting landmarks, like the Statue of Liberty in New York, USA, or the Sydney Opera House, Australia. In this section, we look at long-gone buildings, with four fab facts for our foundations.

TALLEST TOTALLED TOWER

In 2023, the 234-metre-high AXA Tower in Singapore became the world's tallest building to be demolished on purpose. At 305 metres, its replacement will become the city's tallest skyscraper.

TALLEST TOPPLE TOWER

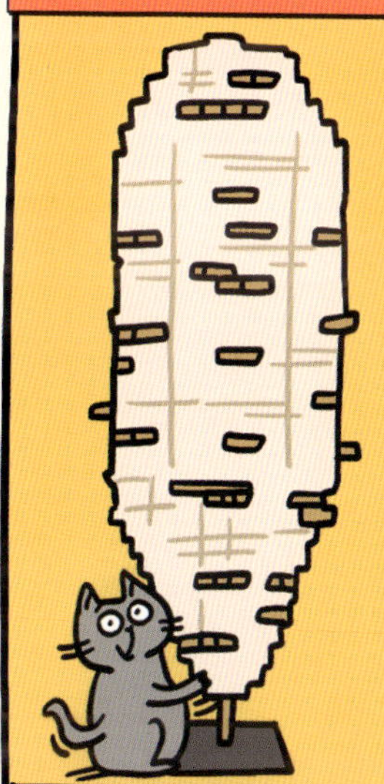

The world record for a tower built from jenga bricks was set in Canada in 2025. At only one metre tall, it contained 3,000 pieces all balanced on a single brick!

MOSTLY MISSING PALACE

The UK's Houses of Parliament in Westminster, London, was home to kings and queens in the Middle Ages. Today, few parts have survived, the oldest being a 900-year-old meeting hall.

FLYING THE FLAG

Great Zimbabwe is a medieval stone city that gave its name to the modern African country of Zimbabwe. Now largely in ruins, its carved stone eagles inspired the one on the national flag!

GREAT LIBRARY

SHELF LIVES

GREAT NEWS

Opened in 2002, the Bibliotheca Alexandrina, Egypt, is a new library to replace the lost one. It can hold up to 8 million books and, unlike the ancient original, it has a planetarium and a dedicated children's library!

WHOLLY HOLY

Egypt is also home to the world's oldest operating library. Founded over 1,400 years ago, the library of the Monastery of Saint Catherine in Sinai has many early religious texts.

FLUSH FICTION

The Beitou branch of the Taipei public library has been built with a living roof that collects rainwater and big windows that save on electricity. Captured rainwater is used to flush the library's loos!

PROUD CLOUD

Many modern libraries are marvels of architecture. Calgary Central Library in Alberta, Canada, was designed to look like a giant cloud and has won many important building awards. It was officially opened in 2018 — by an astronaut!

TOY STORIES

New York's Public Library, opened in 1895, is one of the world's largest, alongside libraries in Moscow, London and Washington DC. However, only New York displays the original soft toys that inspired English author A A Milne to write his Winnie-the-Pooh stories!

CRYSTAL PALACE

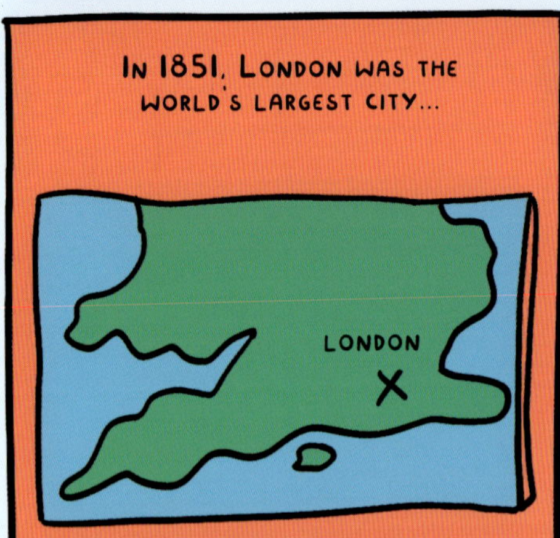

PAST AND PRESENT
PARK LIFE

BADGE OF HONOUR

A Chinese billionaire had plans to rebuild the Crystal Palace, but this hasn't happened yet. Instead, though still a ruin, it gave its name to a major English football team and features on their badge!

ON A ROLL

Bakken in Denmark is the world's oldest amusement park still operating. First opened to the public in 1583, attractions include *Rutschebanen* — a wooden rollercoaster from 1932, whose name means, er, 'rollercoaster' in Danish.

SHOCKING STATE

Taman Festival, on the Indonesian island of Bali is a huge abandoned theme park now overrun by thick jungle. According to local legend, the site is haunted by ghosts and left-behind crocodiles!

COPY THAT!

Opened in 1983, Jaime Duque Park, near Bogotá, Colombia, has model dinosaurs like Crystal Palace, as well as quirky replicas of the Taj Mahal and the Seven Wonders of the Ancient World, including a giant Colossus of Rhodes!

ENNIGALDI-NANNA

ENNIGALDI-NANNA

Hi! My name is Ennigaldi-Nanna. Well, that's one name for me, as I shall explain shortly. As to whether that picture is what I looked like, I can't tell you, but that's how a Mesopotamian priestess may have appeared over 2,500 years ago.

Mesopotamia is the ancient land that lay between the Euphrates river and the Tigris river in areas you humans now call Iraq, Syria and Türkiye. I lived in a city called Ur. No, I haven't forgotten. That really was its name.

I said I was a priestess. Well, I was also a princess. My dad was a king called Nabonidus who ruled Babylon (part of Mesopotamia) from 556 to 539 BCE. He loved to learn about his own kingdom's past and was an early ancient archaeologist.

Loving the past so much, he brought back the role of 'entu' or High Priestess of Ur, a position which hadn't existed for centuries. You had to be female and have royal blood to do it, which is why I got the job.

Sin

My original name was Bel-Shalti-Nannar, but became Ennigaldi-Nanna when, as High Priestess, I became the wife for the moon god Sin. That may sound weird to you, but the Moon and the Sun were very important to ancient peoples.

As the moon-god's wife, I worshipped Sin in the evenings in a small blue room on top of Ur's giant stone temple called a ziggurat. I also had a little office below where I lived and helped run everything religious. Oh, and I had to pray for Dad, too.

Well, Dad's interest in archaeology rubbed off on me, and I began collecting and restoring objects from Mesopotamia's past. I made labels for them using words pressed into wet clay drums and displayed them all in a special building.

A lot later, in 1925 — long after Dad, me and Ur had disappeared — a British archaeologist dug up my collection and realised I had made the world's oldest-known 'museum'. Where my own remains ended up no one knows, but many of my finds are now in a big museum in Iraq's capital, Baghdad. Hooray!

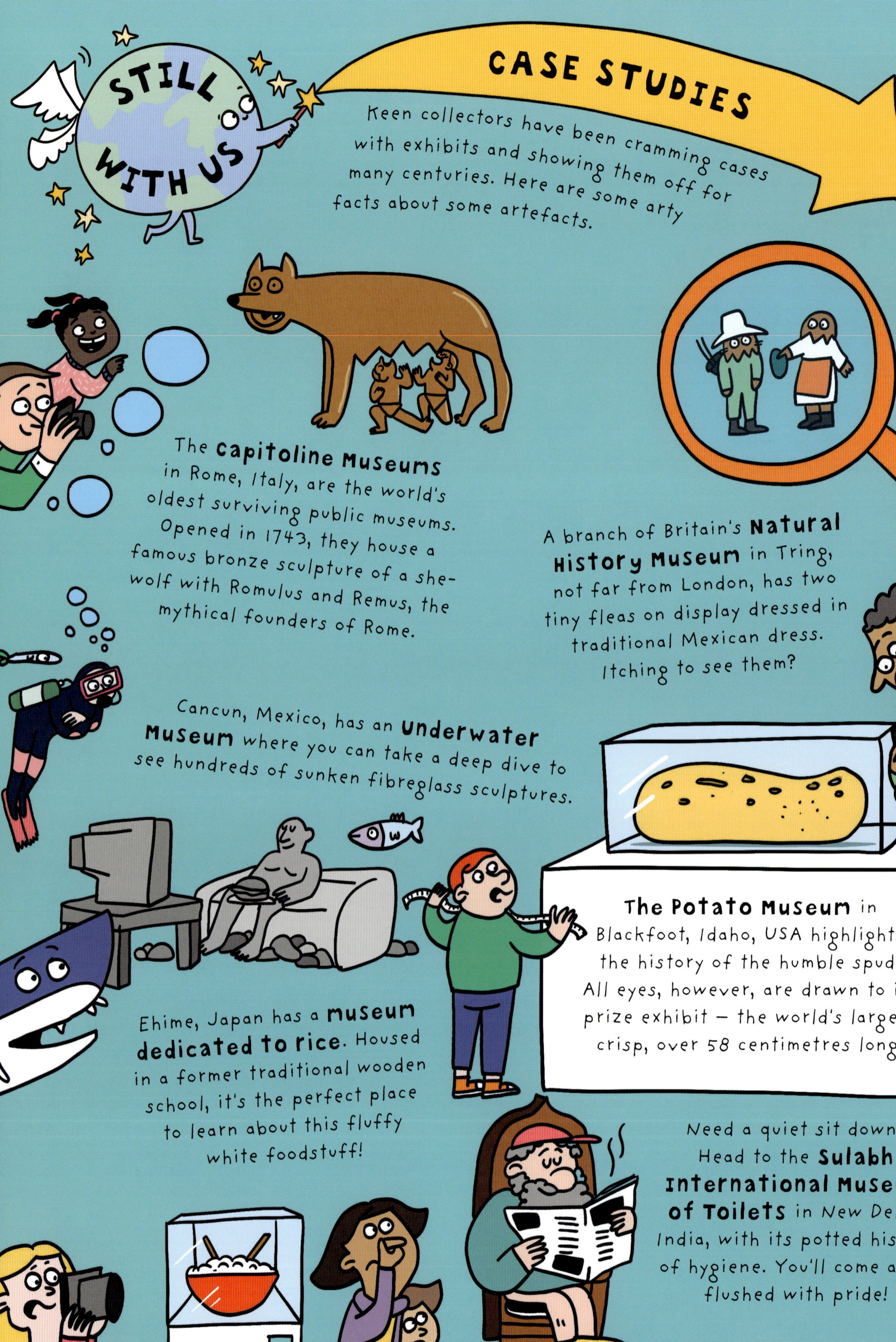

CASE STUDIES

Keen collectors have been cramming cases with exhibits and showing them off for many centuries. Here are some arty facts about some artefacts.

The **Capitoline Museums** in Rome, Italy, are the world's oldest surviving public museums. Opened in 1743, they house a famous bronze sculpture of a she-wolf with Romulus and Remus, the mythical founders of Rome.

A branch of Britain's **Natural History Museum** in Tring, not far from London, has two tiny fleas on display dressed in traditional Mexican dress. Itching to see them?

Cancun, Mexico, has an **Underwater Museum** where you can take a deep dive to see hundreds of sunken fibreglass sculptures.

The Potato Museum in Blackfoot, Idaho, USA highlights the history of the humble spud. All eyes, however, are drawn to its prize exhibit — the world's largest crisp, over 58 centimetres long!

Ehime, Japan has a **museum dedicated to rice**. Housed in a former traditional wooden school, it's the perfect place to learn about this fluffy white foodstuff!

Need a quiet sit down? Head to the **Sulabh International Museum of Toilets** in New Delhi, India, with its potted history of hygiene. You'll come away flushed with pride!

CHAPTER 7
PAST PASTIMES

Humans have occupied Earth for some 300,000 years, and when not busy working to find food and protect their families, have occupied themselves with a vast variety of games, hobbies and artistic interests. This section starts with four fab facts.

OLDEST OLYMPIC EVENT

The longest-running Olympic event is, er, running, seen at the very first games in ancient Greece in 776 BCE. Known as the stadion, the race gave us the word 'stadium'.

DULLEST OLYMPIC SPORT

Many events have been cut from the modern games. 'Plunge for distance' in which swimmers simply drifted from a shallow dive was declared the most boring to watch.

EARLIEST-RECORDED RECORDER

A 60,000 year old flute carved from a cave bear bone dates back to Neanderthal times. Found in Slovenia in 1995, it is the oldest-known musical instrument.

MOST MISSING MOVIE

Many early movies are lost, including a vampire mystery from 1927 called *London After Midnight*. A single surviving film poster sold for $478,000 US in 2014.

GLOBE THEATRE

WILL POWER

RAISING THE ROOF

Shakespeare's Globe is a modern replica of the Globe Theatre, close to its original site. Opened to playgoers in 1997, it was the capital's first — and only — thatched building since the Great Fire of London in 1666.

WHAT'S IN A NAME?

Just six of Shakespeare's signatures have survived. They are all on legal documents and in each instance, Shakespeare — the world's most famous writer — spells his name differently!

TAKE HIS WORD FOR IT!

Shakespeare's plays were published after his death in a book known as the *First Folio*. They included hundreds of words used today, such as kissing, zany and the classic joke set-up, 'Knock, knock...' 'Who's there?'

GIMME SOME SPACE

Shakespeare's plays are still performed on stage and in movies, often with new settings for a contemporary audiences. One famous science fiction film, *Forbidden Planet*, set one of his plays (*The Tempest*) in space and featured a giant robot named Robby!

73

DANCING PLAGUE

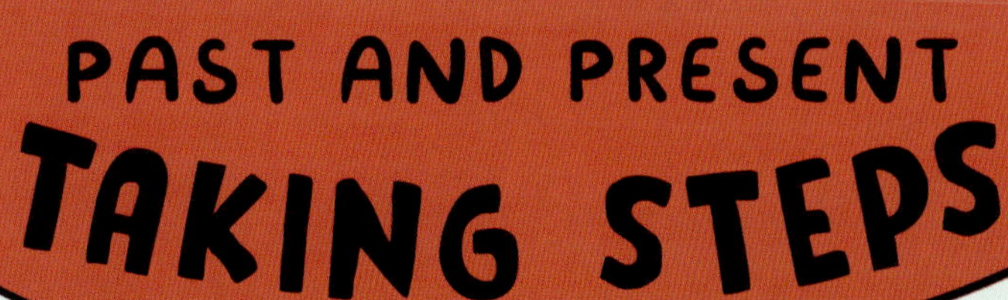

MARATHON EFFORT

Dance marathons were competitions where American audiences watched couples dance non-stop, only getting 15 minutes of rest each hour. In 1933, hairdresser Callum DeVillier and his partner Vonny Kuchinski danced for over five months, becoming world champions and winning $1,000 US.

TWISTY SIXTIES

The rock and roll music of the 1960s inspired many crazy new dances, including the Mashed Potato, the Chicken Walk, the Frug, the Watusi, the Loco-Motion and — most famously — the Twist, which lives on today as a key move in 'Dad-Dancing'.

CRACKER OF A HAKA

The haka is a traditional dance created by the Māori people of Aotearoa (New Zealand). In September 2024, a crowd of 6,531 people performed at Eden Park sports stadium to win back a world record previously held by France.

HOP IT!

In 2012, South Korean K-pop performer Psy released a video for his song 'Gangnam Style' in which he mimed riding a horse while spinning a lasso. His moves were a hit worldwide, but Psy originally considered dancing like a panda or a kangaroo. How does a panda dance?

BIHU-RAY!

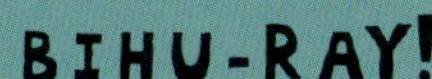

Bihu is a colourful group dance from the Indian state of Assam, where men and women sing and move to the playing of drums. In April 2023, 11,298 people joined in a record-breaking bihu, smashing the former figure of just 500!

'THE CREATURE'

'THE CREATURE'

Hello. I'm 'The Creature'. Not a very flattering name, is it? And that isn't exactly a flattering picture of me, though quite accurate, sadly.

I was created by a 19-year-old woman novelist called Mary Godwin. She fell in love with a famous English poet called Percy Bysshe Shelley, who was already married, causing a big scandal. Although Mary and Percy did later marry.

Mary Shelley

In the summer of 1816, Percy, Mary and her stepsister Claire had a summer holiday on the shores of Lake Geneva in Switzerland. Only it was more like winter than summer, with constant rain, thunder and lightning.

Also staying nearby was another famous English poet, Lord Byron, and his personal physician Doctor Polidori. Bored of being imprisoned indoors by the weather, the group of friends started a contest to come up with a ghost story.

Mary struggled for an idea, until she had a nightmare vision of a mad university student called Victor Frankenstein trying to create a new living person using body parts stolen from corpses and animal slaughterhouses.

You guessed it. That 'monster' was me — 2.4 metres tall, heavily built and with yellow eyes and skin. I was a shocking sight, and my anger at being hated by humans made me kill, though all I really wanted was someone to share my life with.

Mary's monster horror story won among her group of friends, and it was later published as a novel in January 1818 under the title *Frankenstein*. The book made her famous and has been turned into many scary plays, films and TV series over the centuries.

Her story ends with Victor chasing me to the icy seas near the North Pole to try and kill his creation. However, the tables get turned and it is Victor who dies, while I escape over the ice, never to be seen again. (Though you might just want to check under your bed tonight...)

MONA LISA

THE LOUVRE
I'M DESPERATE TO GET TO THE LOUVRE!
ME TOO!
CLENCH!
SINCE THE 19TH CENTURY, THE PAINTING WAS DISPLAYED AT THE LOUVRE, PARIS, FRANCE – THE WORLD'S MOST POPULAR MUSEUM...

TODAY, THIS IS THE WORLD'S MOST FAMOUS ARTWORK...
THE MONA LISA AKA LA GIOCONDA.

IT WAS CREATED OVER 500 YEARS AGO BY BALDY, BEARDY ITALIAN GENIUS LEONARDO DA VINCI.
I'M NO OIL PAINTING - UNLIKE HER!

NOT THAT VISITORS PAID MONA MUCH ATTENTION...
EVER GET THE FEELING YOU'RE BEING WATCHED?
OI! I'M OVER HERE!

THEN, ON 21 AUGUST 1911, THE PAINTING DISAPPEARED.
WE LOST OUR LISA!
GONE!
THE MONA IS A GONA!

THE THEFT WAS WORLD NEWS...
60 DETECTIVES SEEK STOLEN MONA LISA
FRANCE FURIOUS

BIZARRELY, PEOPLE CAME IN HUGE NUMBERS TO VIEW WHERE SHE HAD ONCE HUNG.
GREAT USE OF EMPTY SPACE!
A MASTERPIECE!
STILL GONE!

POLICE HAD MANY SUSPECTS, INCLUDING FAMOUS MODERN ARTIST PABLO PICASSO.
YOU STOLE IT!
YOU CAN'T FRAME ME. I'M INNOCENT!

BUT THE REAL THIEF WAS A GALLERY HANDYMAN CALLED VINCENZO PERUGGIA WHO SMUGGLED IT OUT.
UNDER THE COVER OF MY OVERALLS! HA!
BULGE!

TWO YEARS LATER, HE WAS CAUGHT TRYING TO SELL IT TO AN ART DEALER.
WHAT WILL YOU GIVE ME FOR THIS?
JAIL! YOU'RE NICKED!

BEING STOLEN MADE MONA LISA FAMOUS, BUT ALSO THE SUBJECT OF MANY ATTACKS OVER THE YEARS...
1956
A ROCK
2009
A TEACUP
2022
A CREAM CAKE
2024
SOUP

LUCKILY, SHE IS NOW BEHIND BULLETPROOF GLASS.
DRIP!
STILL SMILING!

PAST AND PRESENT
DISASTERPIECES

SAFETY FIRST

In the 1960s, concerned about further damage or theft, the Louvre looked at getting Mona Lisa insured. She was valued at $100 million US — still a world record for a painting — but they decided it was cheaper to simply improve security precautions.

VALUE: $100,000,000

COMPLETELY ARMLESS

Also on show in the Louvre is the *Venus de Milo*. This ancient Greek marble sculpture was discovered in 1820 and is one of the world's most famous statues, despite missing her arms, a left foot and both earlobes.

MANY HAPPY RETURNS

Dulwich Picture Gallery in south London, UK, has the world's most stolen painting. Their 1632 *Portrait of Jacob de Gheyn III* by Dutch master Rembrandt van Rijn has been stolen — and recovered — four times, earning it the nickname the 'Takeaway Rembrandt'.

GONE DUTCH

The most valuable painting still missing is said to be *The Concert* by another Dutch master, Johannes Vermeer. It was stolen from a US gallery by thieves dressed as police officers in 1990 and is worth at least $250 million US.

MONEY IN THE BANKSY

British graffiti artist Banksy destroyed one of his own artworks by remote control, just after it had been sold at auction for £1.1 million in 2018. The same shredded picture, retitled *Love is in the Bin*, then sold for £16 million in 2021. Go figure!

MYSTERY HISTORY

Some objects from the past continue to baffle boffins as to why they were created. You can see many of them in museums — what remains missing is an explanation of their purpose. Have you a clue to why any of these might have been made?

The Nazca people of southern Peru created **huge figures** in the surface of the desert some 2,000 years ago. Many are in the shape of local plants and animals but, as they are only properly visible from the sky, the reason for the lines is lost.

More than 100 metal **dodecahedrons** — a 12-sided shape with holes — have been found across Europe. Despite dating back to Roman times, none have yet been discovered in Italy, and no one knows what they were made for.

Costa Rica in Central America has hundreds of **giant stone spheres**, some up to 2.5 metres in diameter, crafted and polished smooth over 1,000 years ago. They are now a national symbol of the country but remain a rocky riddle.

Archaeologists in Guanghan, south-west China, have found distinctive masks made by a long-lost culture called the **Sanxingdui** over 3,000 years ago. From the masks' exaggerated features, experts say they may have worshipped eyes, but it's just a guess.

HIT OR MYTH?

Some marvels are missing for a very simple reason:
they never existed in the first place. However, everyone loves
a legend, so in this section we get real and investigate some
famous fables, beginning with four fabulous 'facts'.

WORLD'S BIGGEST MYSTERY?

The so-called 'Bermuda Triangle' region in
the Atlantic Ocean is said to make ships
and aircraft vanish. Aliens and supernatural
forces have been blamed, but regular bad
weather is the best explanation.

MOST BEASTLY BEAST

Medieval scholars loved writing about
unicorns and other mythical animals.
Perhaps the nastiest was the bonnacon,
which was claimed to fire red hot poo
from its rear as a defensive weapon.

BEST SCHOOL PRANK?

In 1994, pupils at a school in Ruwa,
Zimbabwe, claimed a silver UFO had
landed nearby and an alien came out,
leading to mass panic. Later, one 'witness'
confessed that it was just a large shiny
rock that looked like a spaceship.

BIGGEST STITCH UP?

Several major museums around the world
have a 'mermaid' on display. Many were
made in Japan over 200 years ago by
fishermen sewing the head of a monkey
on to the tail of a big fish and sold to
sailors as lucky charms.

KING ARTHUR

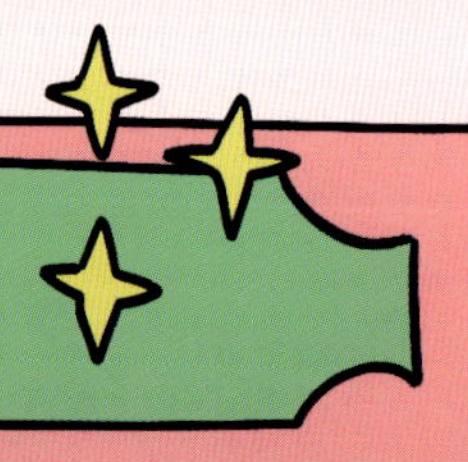

HI! I'M KING ARTHUR.
SHINE!
BUT WAS I A REAL RULER?

SOME CLAIM I WAS A KING OF ENGLAND OVER 1,500 YEARS AGO...
IN A TIME ONCE KNOWN AS THE DARK AGES.
WHO SAID THAT?

SOME USED TO CALL THEM 'DARK' IN PART DUE TO A LACK OF WRITTEN RECORDS.
NO EVIDENCE! WE'RE IN THE DARK HERE.
AND IT'LL TAKE US AGES.
NOTHING!

I FIRST POP UP IN WELSH POEMS ABOUT 594 CE.
CHILD, WHAT RHYMES WITH ARTHUR?
ME, MARTHA!

THEN AROUND 830 CE, A WELSH MONK WROTE A HISTORY SAYING I WAS JUST A SOLDIER, NOT AN ACTUAL KING.
GONE!
I COULD CROWN YOU, MONK!
SORRY...

LUCKILY, 300 YEARS LATER, ANOTHER WELSH WRITER, GEOFFREY OF MONMOUTH, MADE ME A KING AGAIN AND GAVE ME A CASTLE.
THANKS A LOT FOR THE CASTLE, GEOFF!
BACK!
YOU'RE WELCOME.

HE SAID MY CASTLE - LATER NAMED CAMELOT - WAS AT CAERLEON, WALES, WHERE ROMAN RUINS REMAIN TODAY.
ANY CHANCE THIS WAS CAMELOT?
NOT A LOT.

PEOPLE LOVED STORIES ABOUT ME, AND LATER WRITERS KEPT ADDING NEW ELEMENTS...
HOLY GRAIL
MERLIN (THANKS AGAIN, GEOFF!)
ROUND TABLE
PING-PONG TABLE
*NOT THIS ONE
MAGIC SWORD
SIR LANCELOT

BOOKS ABOUT ME BECAME BESTSELLERS IN MEDIEVAL EUROPE - BEATEN ONLY BY THE BIBLE.
THE LATEST KING ARTHUR?
YES, IT'S A LITTLE 'KNIGHT' READING.

STILL, I CAN'T IMAGINE ANYONE IN YOUR TIME READING BOOKS ABOUT WIZARDS, CASTLES, GIANTS, DRAGONS AND MAGIC SWORDS...
CAN YOU?

EXPELLIARMUS!
GONE AGAIN!
OI! STOP THAT!

LIVING LEGEND?

DO NOT DISTURB

Cadbury Castle in Somerset, England, is an ancient hillfort, also said to be the site of Camelot. Legend has it that Arthur and his knights lie sleeping below and come out on Christmas Eve to ride around on invisible horses. Neigh! Surely not?!

TOR STORY

After defeat in battle, Arthur's body supposedly sailed to the mysterious Isle of Avalon. Some say this was Glastonbury Tor, a tall hill once surrounded by water. Monks at the town's abbey later claimed to have found his bones! (See page 23.)

MISSING WIZARD

Tintagel on the coast of Cornwall, England has a ruined castle linked with Arthur, though it was actually built by a rich English prince some time between 1225 and 1233. Merlin the wizard is said to be trapped by magic in a cave below.

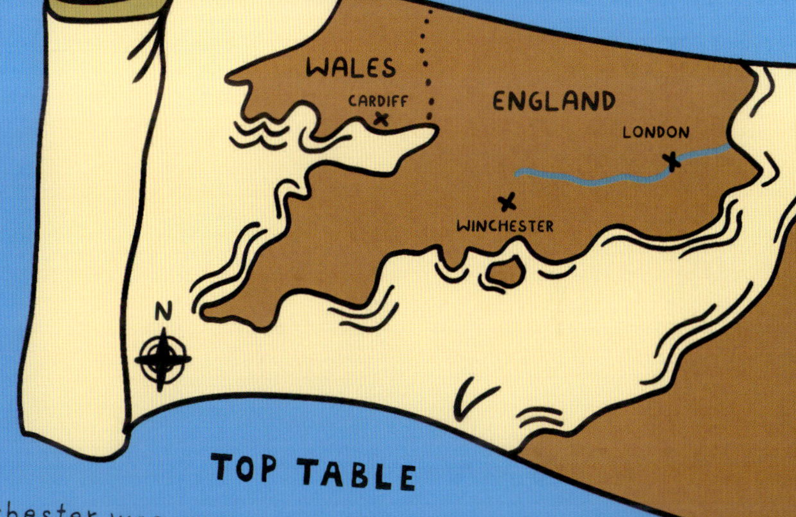

TOP TABLE

Winchester was once an ancient capital in southern England. Inside the city's medieval castle hangs a large round table with an image of Arthur and spaces for 24 knights. It was probably painted in the 1500s and made to celebrate a tournament.

'BIGFOOT'

Hello! My name is, well, I'm not going to reveal it right away. Let's just say for now, you can call me 'Bigfoot' or 'Sasquatch' if you like. And some of you think I probably look like that picture you can see.

I can tell you one thing for an absolute fact: where I live. It's a huge area of remote forested land which spans several states of the USA and the Canadian province of British Columbia — what humans know as the Pacific Northwest — and then some!

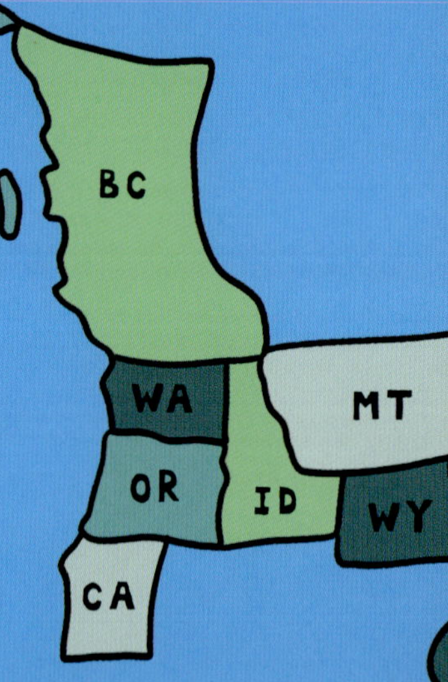

This is a strange thing. It is a rock with a painting on it that some say depicts large, hairy human-like apes. Over 1,000 years old, it was found in California, and made by the Tule River Tribe. Is this a family of Bigfoots? (Or should that be Bigfeet?)

In British Columbia, they prefer the term 'Sasquatch', taken from a local First Nations language. It was used in 1929 for a magazine article about 'hairy giants' who lived in caves and tunnels by a writer called J W Burns.

A big foot

'Bigfoot' came about in 1958. A man called Jerry Crew, working for a logging company in California, discovered giant human-like footprints in the muddy forest floor and a plaster cast of a 40-centimetre-long foot was made. This 'Bigfoot' was big news!

Most famously, a Bigfoot was briefly filmed walking through a remote forest in Northern California in October, 1967. Known as the *Patterson-Gimlin Film* after the pair who shot it, it still remains the best 'evidence' of me after almost 60 years.

But, here's the problem. Those 'Bigfoot' tracks were revealed in 2002 to have been a prank played by a workmate using giant carved wooden feet. Some say the film is just a man in a gorilla suit, and science has never discovered any Bigfoot DNA.

So, who am I really? Probably just one of many American black bears that live in the exact same area as 'Bigfoot'. We can stand on two legs, making us over 2 metres tall, and hairy and scary with it. Sorry about that 'Bigfoot' — missing you already...

A fake foot

The real me

LOCH NESS MONSTER

MONSTER FUN

CHEEKY-NESS

Many hoaxers are still attracted to the loch and its legend. In 1977, an English magician claimed to have summoned the monster from the water with a spell, but his model looked so fake it was dubbed the Loch Ness Muppet!

SILLY-NESS

Nessie photos used to be blurry, black and white blobs, but modern technology is not necessarily better. In 2014, an online satellite map service seemed to show a scary monster looming in the loch. In fact, it was just waves of water made by a boat.

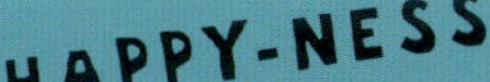

HAPPY-NESS

Nessie-specialist Steve Feltham has been living in a van on the shores of Loch Ness since 1991 — so long that he holds the world record for Nessie-hunting. Determined to debunk fake photos and sightings, he also sells little model monsters to tourists.

LIKE-NESS?

In 2021, British canoeist Richard Mavor was on a charity paddle around Loch Ness, filming his progress with a drone. After posting footage online, someone spotted a strange shape lurking under the water. Guess what — it looked like a plesiosaur!

WHAT A WONDER-FULL WORLD!

This book began with the Seven Wonders of the Ancient World, but Earth has been creating her own marvels from way before we were around. The magnificent seven here were nominated as nature's greatest works — ones which we need to protect to prevent them becoming missing marvels too!

PARICUTIN VOLCANO, MEXICO

This young volcano started appearing in a farmer's field near the city of Uruapan in 1943. It erupted for the next nine years, reaching a height of 424 metres.

VICTORIA FALLS, AFRICA

This massive cascade of water between Zimbabwe and Zambia has many local names, including Mosi-oa Tunya, — meaning 'Thundering Smoke' — from the mist and noise it makes.

RIO DE JANEIRO HARBOUR, BRAZIL

One of the world's largest natural bays was carved out by the Atlantic Ocean and is surrounded by mountains, one with a famous statue on its summit. (See page 59.)

AURORA BOREALIS, ARCTIC CIRCLE
Nicknamed the Northern Lights, these dancing curtains of coloured light are caused by particles from the Sun striking Earth's atmosphere. There are similar displays over the South Pole.

GRAND CANYON, USA
Formed by the Colorado River wearing away its rocks over millions of years, this gigantic groove in the Earth is over 440 kilometres long — more than 10 Olympic marathons.

MOUNT EVEREST, ASIA
On the border of Nepal, at 8,848 kilometres tall, this is the world's highest mountain entirely above the sea. Amazingly, it gets a few millimetres taller every year!

GREAT BARRIER REEF, AUSTRALIA
The world's largest coral reef system, this marine marvel off the Queensland coast is built and maintained by billions of tiny animals all working together.

LOSING IT!

Everyone hates it when things go missing, but it is highly likely that even the most relaxed person might shed tears over losing some of the utterly irreplaceable items here. Some have been missing for centuries, others have only more recently gone astray. Check down the back of your sofa!

CLOWN JEWELS

Legend says Medieval English King John — the Bad King of the Robin Hood tales — lost his realm's original Crown Jewels in the sea off the east of England in October 1216. They were never seen again, but John didn't spend much time worrying about it. He died ten days later.

GOOD EGG

The former Russian Imperial family owned 50 fantastically valuable jewel-encrusted golden eggs, eight of which disappeared in the early twentieth century. Amazingly, one later turned up at a US flea market, where it was bought for $14,000 US — and then valued at a more realistic $33 million US!

MOON MADNESS

On 20 July 1969, about 650 million TV viewers worldwide watched humans walk on the Moon for the first time. Down on Earth, the Apollo II TV transmissions were being videotaped by NASA, but the historic recordings went missing in the early 2000s. One giant fail for mankind!

FOUL PLAY

Men's football teams competing in the FIFA World Cup championship hope to win a shiny gold trophy. The first, introduced in 1930, was known as the Jules Rimet Trophy and displayed in a bulletproof case in Brazil. Despite this, the trophy was stolen in 1983, never to be seen again.

SINKING FEELING

In 1484, in what is now Myanmar, south-east Asia, the Great Bell of Dhammazedi is said to have been the largest bell ever made. It hung in a Buddhist temple until 1608 when it was stolen by a Portuguese warlord. Placed on a raft, it sank into a nearby river and has never been seen — or heard from — since.

CUTTING BLOW

Goro Masamune was medieval Japan's finest sword-maker, and one of his finest blades — the Honjo Masamune — is a Japanese National Treasure. Sadly, it has been missing since the 1940s, when all swords were handed into the police, and it mysteriously disappeared.

LOST FOSSILS

Can you imagine a treasure surviving at least 500,000 years then suddenly going missing? Fossils of an early species of human found in a cave in China did exactly that. The skull fragments and teeth of 'Peking Man' were being sent to the US for safety in 1941 when they disappeared.

BIT OF A DISASTER

Bitcoin is a so-called cryptocurrency — a form of wealth that exists only on a computerised database. In 2013, Welsh computer whizz James Howells had keys to 8,000 Bitcoin on a computer hard drive which mistakenly got sent to a local rubbish dump and lost. Today, they are valued at over £695 million. Oops!

HAPPY LANDINGS

US bicycle-makers Orville and Wilbur Wright made history in December 1903 when their heavier-than-air machine, the 'Wright Flyer', completed the first-ever controlled flight. The nationally important legal document registering their invention went missing in 1980. Incredibly, it was found 36 years later. Phew!

MISSING YOU ALREADY!

Well done on finding your way to the back of this book and not getting lost! But how much can you recall from your journey. Use the clues to jog your memory. If they were like their cousins, the elephants, a mammoth would never forget!

The answers are upside down below. But try not to peek!

ANSWERS

1.GENGHIS KHAN 2.HERCULANEUM 3.AMELIA EARHART 4.MARS
5.BIGFOOT 6.GLOBE THEATRE 7.CRYSTAL PALACE 8.CONCORDE 9.SOLITAIRE
10.PUYI 11.TRABANT 12.TITANIC 13.PERCY FAWCETT 14.HANGING GARDENS
15.ZALMOXES 16.MONA LISA 17.ALEXANDER THE GREAT 18.TEMPLE OF ARTEMIS
19.KING ARTHUR 20.PLESIOSAUR 21.LIGHTHOUSE OF PHAROS
22.COLOSSUS OF RHODES 23.FRANKENSTEIN'S MONSTER 24.GIZA PYRAMID
25.NEANDERTHALS 26.CLEOPATRA 27.PETRA 28.MAUSOLEUM
29.AIRSHIP 30.MAMMOTH

MY SEVEN WONDERS